The Learning Highway

Smart Students and the Net

Trevor Owen & Ron Owston

KEY PORTER  BOOKS

Canadian Catologuing in Publication Data

Owen, Trevor, 1951–
    The learning highway: smart students and the Net

Rev. ed.
Includes index.
ISBN 1-55013-905-3

1. Internet (Computer network). 2. Internet (Computer network) in education. I. Owston, Ronald Davis, 1945– . II. Title.

TK5105.875.I57O84 1997   004.67'8   C97-932727-X

The publisher gratefully acknowledges the support of the Canada Council for the Arts and the Ontario Arts Council for its publishing program.

THE CANADA COUNCIL | LE CONSEIL DES ARTS
FOR THE ARTS | DU CANADA
SINCE 1957 | DEPUIS 1957

Key Porter Books Limited
70 The Esplanade
Toronto, Ontario
Canada M5E 1R2

www.keyporter.com

Design and electronic formatting: Jean Lightfoot Peters

Distributed in the United States by Firefly Books

Printed and bound in Canada

98 99 00 01 02 6 5 4 3 2 1

Table of Contents

The Internet as a "Learning Highway"

Tools of Learning

Learning through Research

Learning through Projects

Acknowledgments

First, we'd like to thank Laurie Coulter, now the Managing Editor at Key Porter, who had the original idea for this book. Thanks as well to Jonathan Webb, who guided the first edition through during his tenure with Key Porter. Their interest in the book certainly encouraged us, and made working with them, and those who followed on subsequent editions, a real pleasure. Our thanks to Susan Renouf and everyone at Key Porter Books in general, and to Michael Mouland for his editorial work on this edition in particular. Thanks as well to Deborah Viets for her thoughtful queries during the final edit.

Much of *The Learning Highway* was developed using the Internet. The "Learning through Projects" section, for example, was developed from calls for participation we posted on the Internet, and we received many more descriptions than we have been able to include here. While we have no way of knowing how many online services actually carried our request, we would like to acknowledge their help in making this project known to those who are already active on the Internet, as well as to everyone who responded—your expressions of interest and support were very encouraging to us.

Finally, we would like to acknowledge and thank the many students who have, and who will, come to know and shape what learning looks like on the Internet. This book is for you.

Everywhere.

Trevor Owen and Ron Owston

CHAPTER 1

Welcome to the Learning Highway

If you are a student in a secondary school, a college or university undergraduate program, or a teacher-education program, then we have written this book for you. *The Learning Highway: Smart Students and the Net* will provide the help you need to use the Internet in your studies—and to use it well. *The Learning Highway* will serve as a bridge between the secondary and post-secondary worlds, preparing students for working online in college or university, and helping you to use your online skills to best advantage with the resources available.

How to Use This Book

A COMPANION GUIDE

The Learning Highway is an educational companion to the many general Internet guides and resource books currently available. Many of these are wonderful books *about* the Internet, including the World Wide Web, making home pages, etcetera, and we recommend that you look at them as well—especially those that will help you gain access *to* the Internet in your area, and help you to understand and use the services at your disposal.

FOCUS ON LEARNING

What we do here, though, is emphasize *how to use the Internet for learning*. In particular, we focus on:

- *why* you might use the Internet for learning,

- *what* you might do online, and,

- *how* you can use the Internet effectively in your studies.

The Learning Highway covers four areas of primary interest to Internet learners:

1. *The Internet as a "Learning Highway"*

   We focus on the Internet as a place of learning rather than as a technology, and offer strategies designed to support your aspirations as Internet learners and to help you express yourself online.

2. *Tools of Learning*

   We focus on the Web-based browser (e.g., Netscape Navigator or Internet Explorer) as the primary tool for learning on the Internet and explore how it is used for multiple functions (i.e., acquiring information on the Web, sending and receiving email, using mailing lists, and participating in newsgroups).

3. *Learning through Research*

We focus on using resources as a means of learning through Internet-based research, and emphasize the process of research rather than the use of a particular illustration or example. Resources and existing sites are cited as examples only.

4. *Learning through Projects*

We focus on how to involve yourself in, or design, your own Internet projects. Our emphasis here is on the design of the various projects described, and in the approaches they take to learning online. Practical examples are given on how these resources may be used to research various topics.

The Learning Highway is designed to help students learn to use the Internet to access relevant and timely sources of information, and to apply online skills for understanding and participating in our increasingly competitive and technological world.

THE INTERNET AS A "LEARNING HIGHWAY"

CHAPTER 2

The Internet as a "Learning Highway"

The Internet as a "Learning Highway"

It's true that there is a lot of information on the *"infobahn,"* but that's only part of the puzzle. What's important for students is that it is a *learning* highway and a pretty super one at that. Human interaction, interpretation, and response are some of the vehicles here, charting a course that begins with ideas and access to information and proceeds to the creation of meaning and new understanding, often undertaken with others who share an interest in the things that interest you. If you have ever wondered what learning on the information highway might actually look like, we hope that the ideas here will help you.

Later on, we will focus on Internet resources and how to find and work with them using Internet software tools that are available through your Web browser. In this section, though, we will look more closely at ways to incorporate the resources that are available to you into your work at school. To do this, we need to address some of the differences between secondary and post-secondary programs, but some of the approaches we explore apply to both, and we want to expose you to them.

APPROACHES FOR SECONDARY AND POST-SECONDARY STUDENTS

We suspect that those of you who are undergraduate students in post-secondary programs will find the resources and tools we examine particularly helpful because much of your school work is likely to emphasize independent or small-group research. As you will see, many Internet resources, and their tools, are well-suited to these approaches. Of course, the Internet is not only for post-secondary students. Nor is it true to say that the only kinds of learning activities that are usefully undertaken online are those based on research and independent work. Not at all.

ONLINE LEARNING PRODUCTIVITY

Indeed, we hope that you will find this book helpful in increasing your "online learning productivity," or what we might describe as your ability to use the Internet to act on your intentions to learn. This applies to all students who use the Internet, no matter what program you are in, whether you are studying at the secondary or post-secondary level, or whether you are conducting research independently or working on a project with people in your classes, around the world, or—most likely—both.

There are also differences between the kinds of resources and tools used at the secondary and post-secondary levels, and in the ways you may use them as well; we want to address these differences in two particular ways.

First, we want to demonstrate the *value* of Internet learning in your own program, so we will address this issue in specific ways both in this section and in the Learning through Projects section. In general, the approach we take here will probably be more familiar to the online experiences of secondary-school students or teacher-education students working at this level because of the classroom-based approach of secondary schools. Accordingly, we discuss the value of working with others and seeing what they do. We also consider how your experience as an online student at one level can inform your learning at another. How, for instance, will your work as an Internet-using student at the secondary level prepare you for learning in post-secondary programs? And if you are one of those lucky post-secondary students who actually used the Internet in secondary school, how can your experiences there help you in your new program? Are these experiences "skills"? If so, are they transferable? It is important to understand how the "independent-research" approach and the "classroom-based" approach interrelate.

At the beginning of this chapter, we noted that access to information on the "infobahn" is only part of the puzzle. We are all familiar with the metaphor of "surfing" the net, which underscores how the Internet may be used to browse, organize, and essentially *acquire* information, but this is only one aspect of how people can use the Internet for learning. We will explore how the Internet can be used to *create* information, both through the expression, or "publication" of one's own learning, as well as through the learning communities in which people become involved. These communities are created largely through shared interests, and the need to know and know more. They are vibrant communities, where concerns about access to reliable sources of information are replaced by participation in what is, in effect, the creation and development of information, or new understanding nurtured through dialogue with interested others. Indeed, many students and teachers have said that learning experiences on the Internet provide them with the opportunity to be taken seriously, because of what they say—in writing—rather than who they may appear to be. People soon learn that this is the case on the Internet, and begin to apply their understanding in many exciting and rewarding ways.

In this section, then, we want to look at some of the ways in which the Internet can be used as a "learning highway," and to do this, we'll focus on some key areas that don't have much to do with technology. Instead, we will concentrate on the main ingredients in building meaning and new understanding, or learning, online.

Human Interaction, Interpretation, and Response

The Internet's learning highway links students and teachers with interested (and interesting) others—across the country, across the street, and around the world. The technology is powerful and may be used to overcome distance and time in ways that are exciting to you as a student—especially when you discover or create projects that apply directly to work you are doing in your classes. A sense of purpose and the desire to understand the needs and experiences of others are the keys to learning on the Internet. To demonstrate, we'll begin to develop this understanding by looking at four areas.

1. TASK AND PURPOSE

Having a clear sense of *task* and *purpose* provides a useful structure and approach to Internet-based learning experiences. We think that the online projects we profile in the last section of the book provide excellent examples. These projects were established—and are often operated—by teachers and other students. Our profiles will offer ideas you can consider for:

- incorporating Internet experiences into courses and assignments;

- helping teachers who don't understand the Internet to consider the value it might have to your work—and theirs; and,

- creating your own projects.

2. WHAT YOUR TEACHERS ARE LIKELY TO NEED

It is important for you to consider what your teachers need—especially if you are farther along in your understanding of the Internet than they are. We will help you to help your teachers by giving you some information that they are likely to find useful.

Of course, many teachers feel comfortable using the Internet for learning—and many are experts in this area themselves. One thing that unites teachers who may be novices with technology and those who may be experts, though, is the fact that they are teachers. So, even if your online abilities and knowledge exceed those of your teachers, they can still assist you. This is especially so when it comes to linking your online activity into course work. Your teachers will know what you need, insofar as their courses are concerned, and will—with a little help from you, in some cases—link what you want to do with what they have to teach you.

3. FOCUS

If you see the Internet as something that provides you with "access to the world…" well, you're right, it does. However, much of the work you can do using the Internet for learning is specific, rather than general. People are drawn to one another through their interests. The ability of the technology to link you to others is exciting, of course, but as anywhere else, meeting people won't be meaningful to you if there is nothing to keep you involved. You will see this for yourself as you begin to find places on the Internet in which to discuss topics of particular interest. We will provide examples of focused activities, drawn from actual projects and experiences that people have set up and/or participated in on the Internet.

4. LEARNING IS NEVER FAR FROM HOME

Remember—learning is something that *you* do. The Internet won't learn for you. But we think you will find that, on the Internet, *everyone* is learning from their experiences with one another. This means, in effect, that what you have to say and to offer others is just as important as what you may get from them. It is the interconnected nature of Internet experiences that gives learning in this forum its active, participatory quality.

What Internet Learners Know Now

It is important to understand how Internet-based experiences draw—and even rely—on your own experience and local setting. Interest has much to do with how people see things. You may think, for instance, that the first snowfall of the year in your area is a typical and rather boring event, but if you are connected to people who never see snow, what you have to say will mean a lot to them. The same can be said of other issues too. Consider these examples: democracy in the South Africa of today, understanding the Holocaust, or exploring your own heritage.

TASK AND PURPOSE

We mentioned that having a task is important to learning on the Internet. However, we know that some of your teachers may not be ready to accept the idea of having to get involved with the technology. This may be out of fear or inexperience, or it may be because teachers are expected to complete certain content requirements in the curriculum, and can't see how what you have to show them might address, inform, or even advance the expectations placed on them. In cases like this, you may find it a hard sell to show them what it is possible to accomplish online.

We think your best chance for success probably lies in demonstrating the value of learning on the Internet through the work produced there, particularly by other students. Are the students who are online now so different from those who are not? We don't think so, but it is true that teachers are often surprised by the work the students produce online, as well as by the involvement they demonstrate in their own learning. We would describe this surprise as having to do with how teachers see students—especially their own students—in new ways. Sometimes this is because the work was not assigned by the teacher, but most of the time, we think it has to do with seeing the value of student work by focusing *on the work*.

What Your Teachers Are Likely to Need

If you are fairly accomplished online now, you might consider preparing your teacher by running a little pilot project that relates to something you have to do for class. Let's say, for example, that you are working on a project about the history of your community and that it involves interviewing senior citizens. You find they share views on some subjects that differ from your own. Using one of the examples or resources mentioned in this book (e.g., a project design or a newsgroup, etc.), post a note or create a Web page in which you solicit the views of people from different communities and/or countries on the topic. It's our guess that what will happen for you is what happens online now for students all over the world, namely, that your understanding of the topic will be enriched by seeing how others interpret and deal with similar concerns in different ways. Print some of the exchanges and show them to your teacher as an interesting complement to your project.

If you do not have access to the Internet, it will likely be helpful to let your teacher know of your interest in using the Internet for learning by emphasizing *what* you want to use the technology for rather than emphasizing the use of the technology itself. We can help you here as well because there are many examples of useful interactions and projects in the pages that follow. You may want to show them to your teacher.

The important point here is that the value of online work is *in the work* more than it is in *using the technology*. Those teachers who may be concerned about their own lack of knowledge in using communications technologies face the prospect of not knowing how they, as your teachers, can help you. Demonstrating the value of Internet-based interactions *through the content of Internet-based material* will help those teachers to make the connection between something they don't know and something they do know—how to teach you.

Teachers want to help you learn. If they realize that learning on the Internet is still learning, they are more likely to respond positively to your initiative, even if they do not possess the skills or knowledge to help you with the technology, or even to understand what it is you are proposing to do. True, following our advice

may mean that you have to insert a few extra steps at the beginning, but don't let this deter you. What you are really doing is helping your teachers learn how they can help you, and most teachers are anxious to do that.

There are issues that teachers often face. Here are some common ones, along with some ideas to help you get started.

MANY WAYS TO LEARN

You have probably noticed that teachers employ various instructional approaches—from lectures in college or university, in which professors impart information to a large group, to cooperative learning strategies that involve people collaborating on tasks in groups. It is also likely that you know teachers who seem to be more comfortable with one approach instead of another. We think it will be useful for you to consider why a particular approach is used in lieu of another, say, group discussion for one kind of activity, direct instruction for another, and then to consider situations in which each of these might be more useful to the learning process. Whatever you decide is useful to us here because the point we want to make has to do with how these ideas appear on the Internet.

INFORMATION AND INTERACTION

By now, everyone is familiar with the phrase "information superhighway." American Vice-President Al Gore coined this phrase to describe the importance of communications technologies to the future of his country. He wished to convey how an "electronic highway" is as important to his country today as a national transportation network of highways was in his father's time (his father played a leading role in developing such a network of highways in the United States of America).

We think the idea of an information superhighway tells only part of the story, because many different approaches can be taken online. We like to think of the Internet as more than just a place to get information, and that one of the best ways to view it is as a place where people interact.

FOCUS

Internet-based activities that you undertake for school should be specific, rather than general. There are several reasons why this approach is important:

Information

Requests for information may provide a useful complement to projects you undertake in school. To have a sense of what it is like to live in an area you are studying or to be connected to someone who has particular expertise in a field you are researching are exciting uses of the Internet. Of course, many of the resources and tools you will read about here will give you access to lots of information without necessarily involving an exchange with anyone else on the Internet. But remember that the Internet is not simply a place where you can get things. It is also a place where you give information to others or create it with them. The perspectives of others can enrich your understanding of whatever topics you are working on—and your perspectives will be useful to them as well.

Response

Remember, though, that people need to see how to respond to your ideas. If you let them know that you are interested in working with someone on a "Bill of Rights for Teenagers,"

rather than just "Teenagers," then they will have a better idea of what you are looking for. If you do not focus your topics well enough, people will be confused.

Interaction

The approaches and possibilities introduced so far in this section suggest that there is value in the kind of interactions and the new ways of working with others that the Internet offers.

With the emphasis we have placed on things such as *task and purpose*, *what your teachers are likely to need*, and having a *focus*, we think that the Internet presents new and useful opportunities for learning.

In the next chapter, we want to look at some ways to understand these opportunities, and to explore concepts that students who want to bring Internet learning to their studies will need to know. We will explore some of these new ways of working together through the experiences people have had learning on the Internet, and through some of the issues they raise.

Key Concepts in This Chapter

- Human interaction, interpretation, and response are some of the keys to learning on the Internet.

- Your "online learning productivity" depends primarily on your ability to use the Internet to act on your intentions to learn, whether you are studying at the secondary or post-secondary level, conducting research independently, or working on a project with people online or in your classes.

- Having a clear sense of task and purpose provides a useful structure and approach to Internet-based learning experiences.

- Consider what your teachers need—especially if you are farther along in your understanding of the Internet than they are.

- Much of the work you can do using the Internet for learning is specific, rather than general.

- People are drawn to one another through their interests. It is the interconnected nature of Internet experiences that gives learning on the Internet its active, participatory quality.

- Internet-based experiences draw—and even rely—on your own experience and local setting. The perspectives of others can enrich your understanding of whatever topics you are working on—and your perspectives will be useful to them as well.

- The value of online work is in the work more than it is in using the technology.

- Teachers want to help you learn, and know how to help you—even if your own knowledge of the Internet exceeds theirs.

CHAPTER 3

Changing Roles

Like most of the people who read this book, teachers are often quite excited by the possibility of using computer-based communications technologies for learning. One of the authors of this book was a teacher who saw that the opportunities to extend the reach of his classroom would offer experiences that were not readily available to his students, and he wanted to pursue those opportunities. However, when Trevor Owen set out to introduce online learning experiences at his school, he ran into several problems. First, the school was not well-equipped to deal with the concept of communications technologies in education, let alone to put students online. There were worries about spending money on such an effort without proof that learning would be enhanced. But even though the hurdles of obtaining access to computers and modems and installing phone lines existed, the most compelling difficulty was the concern of his colleagues.

"Many teachers on staff were concerned that they didn't know the technology, and, like most teachers, that they were already overloaded with work. Not surprisingly, there was a good deal of resistance to the idea that online activity might be added to the curriculum. In the end,

we made a deal—I promised not to bug them to participate; they promised not to stand in my way."

It wasn't long before it became clear that he had a problem. The online exchanges were wonderful, and Owen wanted his colleagues to see what was happening.

> Over the year, I printed up some of the online exchanges and left them on the lunch table in the staff room. I didn't say a thing about them, having promised not to bug people, and just left them there for anyone to read if they felt like it.

> They did, and many teachers were surprised at the quality of the exchanges. They commented that they hadn't realized the depth and breadth of some of the students' thinking—and many were their own students too. By the end of the year, many of my colleagues wanted to know more about getting online.

The moral of this anecdote is the idea we introduced in the last chapter—that the value of the work lies in the work itself. The online forum provides a way, or a set of ways, in which to see things differently than we do now.

This is both useful and troublesome for teachers, and it will be both useful and troublesome for you who, as students, want to incorporate Internet-based experiences in your studies.

Singed Sheep Head

We'd like to illustrate this idea with an example drawn from Owen's experience. One day, an online message arrived in class. It was from two students who were younger than the students in his class, but as you will see, that didn't really matter.

> Hi, Riverdale,
>
> We are two girls in Olafsfjörður, our names are Auður and Erla. Auður is 13 years old, 149 centimeters and 32 kilos. Her hair is short and blonde. She wears glasses. Her shoe number is 35. Her birthday is the 12th. of February. She has got two sisters and two brothers, but they have all left home. Her mother works in a shop and her father is a teacher. Her favourite subjects are Maths, Danish and Gymnastic. Her hobbies are tennis, football, volleyball, skiing, billiard and many more. Her favourite groups are Simply Red, Peter Cetera and Rod Stewart.
>
> Erla is 14 years old, 163 centimeters and 52 kilos. Her hair is long and blonde. Her shoe number is 37. Her birthday is the 18th. of January. She has got two sisters. One is 15 and the other is

> 10. Her mother is a nurse and her father is a mechanic. Her favourite subjects are tennis, football, skiing, billiard and many more. Her favourite groups are Simply Red, Rod Stewart, George Michael and all those who sing or play slow songs.
>
> What actor do you prefer? We like Tom Cruise, Michael J. Fox and Lou Diamond Phillips.

There is more to this note, which we will look at shortly. But first we want to point out that many email exchanges on the Internet—especially initial exchanges—look like this. They are filled with specific details, often with introductions that focus on physical appearance. And they often come in class sets. Now, just imagine what it would be like to receive online messages from everyone in a class with information about "shoe numbers." It's not terribly exciting, and there is really no reason to expect that it should be—after all, once is fine, but almost nothing is that exciting thirty odd times!

Fortunately, in this case, there was more to the message from Auður and Erla. If you read the following passage, a difference will emerge, both in the content of the message and in the interest it is likely to generate.

> We are in 8th grade and in our school there are 15 boys and girls. We do not wear school uniforms. We learn three languages, English, Danish and Icelandic.
>
> Our country is quite small and the inhabitants are about 250.000. The

country is very high and there are many glaciers. The biggest one is Vatnajokull (Waterglacier) and it is the biggest one in Europe. There are not many woods in Iceland, most of the growth are birch-trees. There are not many wild animals here in Iceland: mice, rats, foxes, minks and reindeers.

Now is a time we call the "slaughtering time." At this time the sheep are slaughtered. We make two kinds of sausages of them, one is mainly blood and also meal and suet of a sheep, then we mix it all together and put into paunches and sew for the opening. The other one is made of liver, kidneys, meal and suet, and put in the paunches too. We eat singed heads and legs of sheep. You maybe think it is disgusting but we like it, especially the singed head.

Our town is in northern Iceland. It is quite small (only ca. 1200 inhabitants). It is surrounded by mountains on three sides and sea at one side. We like living here because it is quiet and the air is quite clean.

This summer we painted ships. There are not many work opportunities here for kids, only town work, baby-sitting and fishing plant. In the ship painting we had

245 kr (that is about 3 pounds) per hour. How much money did you earn this summer?

We would love to receive a letter from you.

Best regards,

Auður and Erla.

Needless to say, this message sparked considerable interest in Owen's class. "Singed sheep head? My students were as excited and curious as they were disgusted by the very sound of such a delicacy."

As it turned out, this interest sparked a relationship that lasted for some time online—as well as in the conventional mail.

"We received the first message at the beginning of December, just before exams and the break for the holidays," Owen recalls. "When I returned to school after the holidays, I found a note in my mail box. It was from the Post Office, letting me know there was a package waiting to be picked up."

The package was from Auður and Erla. It contained, among other things, a few bags of fish chips (remember the fishing plant?), some school newspapers (in Icelandic) and, in the bottom of the box, a small tin. Singed sheep head. "Everyone in the class was invited to try the Icelandic delicacy," Owen says, "and afterwards, the class decided to put together a return package with information about our own school, and a selection of foods from the various nationalities represented in our multicultural class."

USEFUL DETAILS

There are some points we want to make with this example. First, useful Internet exchanges are characterized by details, but not just any details. There were many details in the example from Auður and Erla, but only some of these interested Owen's class. The physical descriptions of age and hair color, for instance, were not of particular interest. However, the details about making the sausages, and especially about the singed sheep head were much more interesting. And, in the end, they told us a good deal not only about life in Olafsfjörður and how it is likely quite different from yours, but also a good deal about Auður and Erla.

We know, for instance, the music groups they liked when they sent that message, the particular things they liked to do, subjects in school, and so on. But there are things we come to know about their character as well, by the ways they convey their ideas. We especially liked the way they had a little fun with their stories of the sausage-making and the singed sheep head. It's clear that they knew how non-Icelanders in Canada would react to the story of the sheep head. "You may think it is disgusting," they write, "but we like it, especially the singed head." We can tell from this that Auður and Erla like to have some fun, and that they know how to convey this to others as they write about aspects of their culture.

There is a simple but powerful message here. It isn't just where you are from or how you can use technology that matters. It is what you have to say that really counts. Your own way of expressing your experiences is very important when it comes to learning on the Internet.

CLASS OR GROUP ASSIGNMENTS

Generally speaking, as we have already noted, class or group assignments and activities should not be too narrow in their focus. If you are going to include "useful details," in which you draw on your own experiences to offer perspectives and ideas on the purposes of your interactions with others, then also keep in mind that these should be varied enough to interest the audience you want to communicate with.

We recommend that you look at your assignments with a view to including whatever information is necessary, of course, but with the benefit of your comments and perspectives as well. As you saw in the example from Iceland, it was really the comments and perspectives that Auður and Erla brought to the exchange that created interest. What *you* bring to an exchange provides a good deal of the authenticity people feel they acquire from Internet-based experiences.

WHO DECIDES?

Remember that although your Internet projects are *sustained* by technology, they are not really *about* technology. It is what you have to say on the Internet that counts, not how you got it online. This is an important aspect to learning on the Internet, although we do want to point out that technology does have an impact on who controls what is seen and considered in courses.

Who, for example, decided to include the message from Auður and Erla in the course? The teacher? It could have been, but only if he had received it first. In many classes the teacher has access to all exchanges before the class does. But in other classes the students have direct access to material and may see it before the teacher.

We want to consider the situation described in the second instance because the relationship between student and teacher can change quite radically online, and it may be the case that neither your teachers nor you have considered the impact of this change on the courses in which both of you are involved.

Control

WRITERS IN ELECTRONIC RESIDENCE

To illustrate this point, we are going to draw on another real example. This one is from one of the projects we will look at again later, the *Writers in Electronic Residence (WIER)* program. WIER is an online project that uses the Internet to link students and teachers with professional writers in Canada. Students post original writing, usually poetry and short prose works, for comment by writers, teachers, and other students in a computer conference. In some schools, the material is handled by the teacher, or perhaps a student assistant or group of assistants, and made available to others in print form. In other schools, students have direct access to the material, so it is possible for them to see writing and exchanges before the teacher does.

This happens regularly in WIER and teachers who operate the program this way are prepared to deal with the work that comes. There have been several cases in which this approach has tested the conviction of teachers, though, and we would like to highlight one of them.

One warning—the piece that follows is power-ful and may offend some. We think it is important that you read it, though.

INBORN CONSENT

One day, schools participating in the secondary and college levels of WIER found the following poem waiting for them online:

inborn consent

Hey Bitch—
   wanna fuck?

Hey Bitch—
   yeah you!
   wanna fuck?

I know you do
   you yelled it to me
   with your slutwalk

you screamed
   your obscene desire to me
   with your whoreclothes

Hey Bitch—
   wanna fuck?

I don't give a shit
   that your girlvoice
   whispers no

Your womanbody already
   said yes

—Delacey Tedesco

When you read the poem "inborn consent," what was your reaction? Take a moment now to record some of your first thoughts. Feel free to read the poem several times and record your responses as you do.

When you have done this, look at the comments that follow. They are a small sampling of the responses that appeared online:

> Your poem reminds me of the lyrics to quite a few of the RAP songs currently popular. The difference is, minus the beat, the aggression of the singers, the erotic posing of the dancers and models, the irritating zooms and close-ups, your verse feels ironic, as though the words are turning back against the speaker.
>
> I don't mean that there isn't some truth in the speaker's words: we can see blooming sexuality in girls/young women & sometimes they are unsure of how to handle their own attractiveness.
>
> Why that means people like having some guy shout "yo a ho'" in their faces, I don't know.
>
> I'm getting off topic. Your poem doesn't do any of those things. It does a good job of recreating a certain kind of voice. I think it feels like an ironic depiction. Is that how you mean it?

•

> Honestly, I find this offensive and unacceptable. It makes sense, I see your point, but I don't think that this sort of language is necessary. Of course, there is still poetic license and all and I myself wrote a poem saying that the poem is for the writer and nobody else, so.... I suppose we need questionable stuff like this to define what "acceptable" is. I don't know what else to say. If you don't like it, don't read it, right? So I won't.

•

> I fully agree with the point that you are trying to make, if I'm right. What I think you are trying to show is how people (men) judge others by just looking at them (women). I do believe that you could have used a better selection of words. However, your way of putting it creates the realism of first impressions.

•

> I truly want to congratulate you on your sincere portrayal of some male attitudes towards women. I don't think your poem is offensive or gross at all—except perhaps to those who actually think this way. Poems were made to change the world. Maybe this one will make a difference.

•

> Make poems that change the world. That's really nice.

One of the points we want to make using the example of "inborn consent" is that its author, Delacey Tedesco, is the person who decided to post it online. Not the teacher. And in secondary-level classrooms across Canada, "inborn consent" appeared in the same way that any other piece of writing appears in the program—with the blessings of the teacher if the teacher got it first and allowed it to be presented to his or her class, or without the blessings of the teacher, if students happened to get to it first. This presents a real issue for students and teachers when it comes to considering what learning on the Internet looks like.

In this example, though, we want you to focus on issues teachers face. There are several reasons for this. First, the ideas you develop for learning on the Internet may present possibilities for learning that you hadn't considered. Second, the ideas you come up with may present some possibilities for learning that your teacher hadn't considered either. We think that students and teachers need an opportunity to respond to ideas and to think them through in the context of real situations. After all, not all courses are alike.

In most cases, though, the teacher plans and prepares what content will be covered and when and how it will be covered. Students may expect that their teachers are prepared to present material based on the teacher's own knowledge and preparation of that material. In the case of "inborn consent," though, the teacher may not have had the opportunity to prepare, at least not in the sense of preparing a lesson. This change alters the conventional relationship between student and teacher because both are placed in the role of learner.

Participation in online events, like reading and discussing "inborn consent," demonstrates that learning on the Internet applies to everyone—students and teachers. In this example, teachers, students, and writers considered both the poem and the issues raised by the poem. In doing so, they also considered the ideas and issues raised by one another. In short, through direct participation, everyone was learning.

Here's what happened. At first, many people wanted to know whether Delacey was a male or female name. They felt having this information about the author would make a difference to how the poem should be interpreted. Others felt it didn't matter and that the issues raised by the poem were important enough to stand on their own, without regard for the gender of the author. A number of people felt that the issue of the poem was misogyny, and that this overshadowed what the author may have been trying to get from WIER in the first place—a sense of the poem's value as a piece of writing, or comments from other writers that might have focused on its form.

The discussion about "inborn consent" ran for two months, involving many students, teachers, and writers across the country. All could be said to have been engaged in the act of learning. And we know from the exchanges that the discussions everyone saw online took place first in classrooms, among people who knew one another in the context of daily school life.

Now, refer to the notes you made about "inborn consent." Do you have thoughts to contribute to the discussion? Did any of the other comments you read about the poem change your thinking in any way? How might the discussion have evolved if your contribution had been part of it? It's our guess that you did have some thoughts, and that you could have contributed them to this discussion. We think it is this involvement that qualifies you as an Internet learner, not whether you use, or even like, computers.

WIER is one of the projects we report on in the Learning through Projects section, so we'll look at it in more detail there. For now, though, we want to consider some of the elements that appear among students and teachers as they encounter one another in ways that were not possible before they began to work together online. In the next chapter, we'll explore how some of these elements, which often appear in various online programs, demonstrate the value of the Internet as a learning highway.

Key Concepts in This Chapter

- Useful Internet exchanges are characterized by details, but not just any details.

- You can draw on your own experiences to offer perspectives and ideas on the purposes of your interactions with others.

- Your Internet projects are sustained by technology, but they are not really about technology. It is what you have to say on the Internet that counts, not how you got it online.

- Technology has an impact on who controls what is seen and considered in courses.

CHAPTER 4

You Are What You Say You Are

What a WONDERFUL learning experience it has been. It has given me a new perspective on learning, and learning how to learn. With other writers of the world, we have all responded and contributed to one another. I see this as something that has changed my life.... Education shouldn't always be within classroom walls.

—Yit Yin Tong

We want to discuss "being what you say you are." To do this, we need you to participate in an experiment. Take a piece of paper and a pen or pencil so you can jot down a few notes. Look at this page, and take thirty seconds to write down everything you notice about Yit Yin Tong. When you are done, read on for more instructions.

Now cover page 19 with your piece of paper so that only Yit Yin Tong's picture is showing. Look at her picture and jot down everything you notice about her now—but include only what you haven't already written.

When you've finished, cover her photo so that only her comment appears. Once again, jot down everything you notice about Yit Yin Tong now.

Were the things you wrote down without Yit Yin Tong's picture different from the things you wrote down when you had the picture and the text, or when you had the picture alone? If so, you are like most people. Generally speaking, when this experiment is done, people tend to notice the same things. When presented with both the picture and the text, people tend to jot down the things they noticed about Yit Yin Tong that are based on visual information. They note, for instance, that she is female, that she seems happy, that she wears glasses, and that she appears to be Asian. Often they notice other things too, such as the earphones she seems to be wearing. (In fact, she is hard of hearing and wears a "phonic ear" system to hear better.)

When her picture is covered up people tend to notice other things about Yit Yin Tong. They notice that she is emphatic and excited, from her writing "WONDERFUL" in capital letters. They notice that she seems to enjoy learning ("It has given me a new perspective on learning …") and that this is important to her ("… and learning how to learn.") And they see other things too; for example, she views herself as a member of a community of writers ("With other writers of the world …") who values

working with others ("… we have all responded and contributed to one another"); that she reflects on her experiences ("I see this as something that has changed my life."); and that she is prepared to see things in new ways as a result ("… education shouldn't always be within classroom walls.")

It's not surprising that this happens, because the way in which you get to know someone is different online than it is face-to-face. Your attention is drawn to different things and, in this case, the things that are available are the things that people say in their writing. We think Yit Yin's online experience serves as another example of how, on the Internet, you are what you say you are.

There are many ways to use the Internet to interact with other people, but for us, this is one of the most compelling. Throughout the rest of this book, we will consider others, such as how learning from the *process* of undertaking research on the Internet is just as important as learning from the *results* of it. We'll look at projects people have created that serve as examples of how important the exchange of *ideas* is to people, and how this sense of importance is what makes learning on the Internet so exciting and worthwhile.

In the next section, though, we want to look at Internet tools and how they can be used as tools of learning.

Key Concept in This Chapter

- On the Internet, you are what you say you are—something that is likely to alter how people know you, and how you know them.

TOOLS OF LEARNING

Introduction

To navigate the learning highway all you need to know is how to use one essential tool—the Web browser. The latest Web browsers contain the components necessary to view documents, graphics, and video, listen to music, download software, send and receive email, and participate in Internet newsgroups. This is a far cry from only a few short years ago when you needed to master several separate software packages and learn some fairly arcane lingo to be able to use the Internet effectively for learning.

In this section, we'll explain how to use the various components of Netscape Navigator, the most widely used Web browser. Our illustrations will show Navigator version 3.0 for the Macintosh.* Whether you have the Macintosh or Windows version of Navigator doesn't really matter when you read this section as there are only minor differences between the two. Nor do you need to be concerned if instead you have one of the other popular browsers, such as Microsoft's Internet Explorer, because the principles of operation of all common browsers are the same.

We'll begin the section with an explanation of how to browse the Web with Navigator. Following this, we'll describe how to use Navigator's email and newsgroup features. Our discussion will assume that you already have a Web browser installed on your computer and that you have a connection to the Internet.

---

* At the time of writing Netscape released version 4.0 of its browser. Although this version has some additional features and enhancements, all of the principles discussed in this section are equally applicable to version 4.0.

CHAPTER 5

How to Browse the Web with Netscape Navigator

In this chapter, you'll learn all you need to know to browse the Web with Netscape Navigator. We'll describe Navigator's window, how to access any Web site, retrieve Web pages, and customize its features.

Anatomy of Navigator

When you launch Netscape Navigator, you'll see a window similar to the one on the next page. Across the very top of the window is a row of names of pull-down menus just as in any other computer application, such as a word processor. These menus contain all of the commands necessary to operate Navigator. Immediately below the pull-down menu names is the *toolbar*. The toolbar provides convenient access to the most commonly used commands by allowing you to just click on an icon rather than pulling down a menu to make a selection. Beneath the toolbar is the *location line*, which tells you the address, known as the *Uniform Resource Locator* (URL), of the Web page you are currently viewing. The row of buttons below the location line, called *directory buttons*, quickly take you to Web pages that Navigator's developers think you'll want to use often.

The central part of the window displays a Web page, also referred to as a Web document. Its name is shown at the very top of the window following the word "Netscape." Each time you launch Navigator you are taken to Netscape Corporation's *home page* by default, or to a home page that you have specified. A home page is somewhat like the cover of a book. It typically provides the name of a Web site, an introduction to its contents, and links to other pages at the site or to other sites. Frequently you'll find that one or more words on a Web page are underlined. The underlining indicates a *hyperlink*. You'll notice that when you move your mouse pointer over a hyperlink, the *status line* at the very bottom of the window shows the URL of the hyperlink. When you click on a hyperlink, the status line tells you that you are connecting to that URL and gives you an indication of how quickly the new page is loading. After the page is fully loaded, the word "Done" appears in the status line. When you return to the original page, you will discover that the color of the hyperlink has changed. This helps you keep track of which pages you have already viewed.

Browsing the Web with Navigator

BASIC NAVIGATION TECHNIQUES

Clicking on hyperlinks as we just described is one way to browse the Web with Navigator. Sooner or later you will want to return to a page you looked at before and then perhaps jump ahead to another page you've also viewed. You can do this by clicking on the **Back** and **Forward** arrows at the left of the toolbar.

Choosing Back and Forward from the **Go** pull-down menu accomplishes the same thing. Another way to move back and forward is to hold down your mouse button anywhere in Navigator's window and a pop-up menu will appear from which you can select either navigation command.

If you've viewed many different pages and want to quickly return to one of the earlier ones you've seen, clicking on the arrows can be very tedious. Fortunately, Navigator makes this task simple by providing you with a list of pages you've recently viewed. You can see this *history*

Go	**Bookmarks**	**Options**	**Directory**	**Window**	
Back					⌘ [
Forward					⌘]
Home					
Stop Loading					⌘ .
✓ **HotBot**					⌘ 0
Welcome to Lycos					⌘ 1
Infoseek					⌘ 2
AltaVista: Main Page					⌘ 3
Yahoo!					⌘ 4
York University Faculty of Education Home Page					⌘ 5

list by pulling down the Go menu again as shown above.

When you select any item on the list, you'll immediately be taken to that page. The names in the history list are obtained from the page titles. Web authors sometimes don't title their pages accurately, so be warned that from time to time you'll see titles that provide no clues whatsoever to a page's content.

To get back to the home page that you saw when you started Navigator, you can select Home from the Go menu or simply click on the Home icon on the toolbar.

THREE WAYS TO GET TO A URL
Now suppose a friend has given you the address of a "cool" Web page you want to view or you want to check out a Web site that you've read or heard about. You can access the page directly by entering the URL into Navigator. There are three ways to do this:

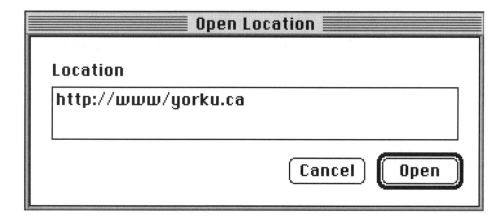

1. Click on the **Open** icon of the toolbar, enter the address in the dialog box, and click **OK**. (The dialog box is shown on page 25.)

2. Select **Open Location** from the File pull-down menu and proceed as above.

3. Replace the address in the location line with the address you want to go to and press the Return key.

In theory, when you enter a URL, you should copy it exactly as you see it written, paying attention to upper- and lower-case letters; however, in practice, you'll find that very few URLs are case sensitive, so you can enter them all in lower-case to make the typing easier. If you encounter a URL that doesn't work, try entering it exactly as you saw it written in case it is an exception.

You don't need to enter the **http://** part of a URL because Navigator assumes that's what you want if it is omitted. Also, if you want to go to a commercial Web site, most of the time you only need to enter the name of the site because Navigator will automatically add **http://www** in front of the name and **.com** at the end. For example, to go to **http://www.yahoo.com**, simply enter **yahoo**.

One other pointer we'd like to offer is that you watch for the tilde character (~) because it frequently occurs in URLs and you may confuse it with a hyphen (-). The tilde, which is found in the upper left-hand corner of most keyboards, is often used to denote the home directory of a person on a Web server that is used by many people. For example, the URLs of our home directories on the server we use are **http://www.edu.yorku.ca/~towen** and **http://www.edu.yorku.ca/~rowston**.

OF CLIENTS AND SERVERS

Throughout this section we'll talk about Internet servers—mail servers, mail list servers, newsgroup servers, and Web servers. Servers are powerful computers with large hard disk capacities. They sit, connected to the Internet, waiting patiently to be contacted by other computers, called clients, to deliver data to them. For example, when you are connected to the Internet and running Netscape Navigator, your computer becomes a Web client. Every time you click on a hyperlink or enter a URL, you send a message to a Web server that then delivers the data you requested back to you.

WORKING WITH BOOKMARKS

The history list provides a record of the sites you've visited since you last launched Navigator. Therefore, once you quit Navigator the names in the history list will be lost. To keep a permanent record of pages you may want to return to sometime in the future, you

Bookmarks	Options	Directory	Window
Add Bookmark			

RealAudio Home Page
York University Faculty Association
Search tools
Tools
Directories
Teaching Resources
Msc
Theoretical Sources in IT
ILTweb: LiveText: Index
Libweb – Library WWW Servers
CARRIE: An Electronic Library

WHAT EXACTLY IS A URL?

A URL is the Internet's version of a ZIP or postal code. Every resource that's available on the Internet has a unique URL so that it can be located from anywhere in the world. Shown below is a typical URL.

http://www.myschool.edu/student/ anyname.html

URLs consist of three main parts. The first part, **http://**, which is called the *protocol*, indicates what kind of resource is to be found at the location. Most often you'll see **http** (Hypertext Transfer Protocol, which indicates a Web resource). Other protocols you'll see are Telnet, Gopher, FTP (File Transfer Protocol, the protocol used for uploading and downloading files on the Internet), and News (for accessing newsgroups).

Next to the protocol is the *domain*, **www.myschool.edu**, which identifies the computer where the resource is to be found. Every computer connected to the Internet has a domain. Sometimes you'll see the domain represented as a number, such as 130.63.218.180. Actually every domain starts as a number and a name is then assigned to it because names are easier to remember than numbers. For example, the name **www.edu.yorku.ca** is assigned to the number 130.63.218.180. When you see only the number it is simply because the owner of the domain hasn't registered a name for that particular number.

The rightmost part of the domain, **edu** in this example, is called the *top-level domain*. This part is of particular interest because it indicates the type of organization that owns the computer where the resource is found. As you might expect, **edu** signifies an educational institution; **com** is for commercial organizations; **gov** is for government; **org** for various kinds of organizations, mainly non-profit ones; and **net** for computer networks. Only the U.S. makes the distinction among the types of organizations in the top-level domain; other countries normally have a country code for all types of organizations, such as "ca," for Canada, "fr," for France, and "au," for Australia.

To the right of the domain is the *directory* in which the resource is located (**/student**), followed by the actual name of the resource (**anyname.html**). If you use a Windows computer, you'll recognize the directory as the path name for a file. Macintosh users should think of the directory as the folder or subfolder in which a file is located. Files frequently have the extension "html" or "htm," which indicates to your Web browser that the document is coded in *Hypertext Markup Language (HTML)*. HTML is a special set of codes inserted into a document that tell a Web browser how to display it.

can tell Navigator to make a *bookmark* for the page. (Internet Explorer calls bookmarks "favorites.") A bookmark is Navigator's equivalent to folding the corner of a page of a book so that you can get back to it conveniently.

You make a bookmark for any page you are

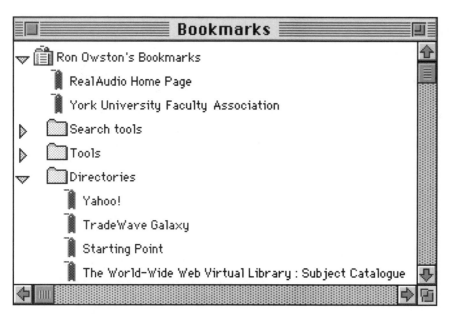

viewing simply by selecting **Add Bookmark** from the **Bookmarks** pull-down menu illustrated on page 26. The name of the page will then appear in the Bookmark menu. Just as with the history list, the bookmark name is determined by the page name. You can rename bookmarks if you go to the **Window** pull-down menu and

---

ORGANIZING YOUR BOOKMARKS

When you first start browsing the Web, you'll find yourself wanting to bookmark just about every page that appears even remotely interesting. Try to avoid this. If you're not selective, you'll soon discover that your list becomes unwieldy and not very helpful. One way to deal with a long list is to take the time to delete bookmarks that you won't likely use and sort the remaining ones into several folders whose names describe their contents.

---

select Bookmarks. You'll then see your complete list of bookmarks. Highlight the name of a bookmark in the list and select **Edit** from the **Item** pull-down menu. You'll then see a box into which you may enter a new name for the bookmark. You may also change the order of any bookmark in the list by first highlighting it and then, while holding the mouse button down, dragging it to another position.

While you're looking at the Item menu, note that there are several tools for organizing your bookmarks, such as sorting them or putting them into folders. To delete a bookmark, however, you have to highlight the bookmark, go to the Edit pull-down menu, and select **Delete Bookmark.**

Retrieving Web Pages

While bookmarks are a handy way to get back to a page you've seen, sometimes when you're

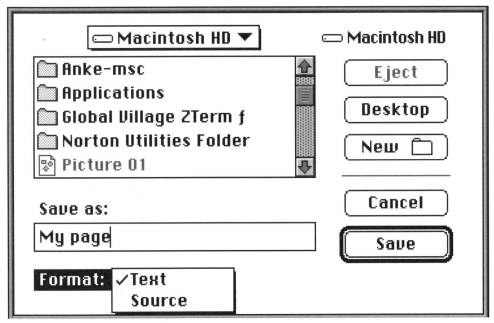

doing research on the Internet, you'll find it more convenient to retrieve a Web page and store it on your computer's hard disk for later viewing. This is particularly true if the page has lots of detailed information that you want to study and you want to minimize your connect time to save money.

To retrieve a page you are currently viewing, go to the **File** pull-down menu and select **Save as**. You'll then be presented with a window, like the one above, that allows you to save the page under whatever directory and file name you want. Note also that you are given a choice to save it either in *source* or *text* format.

If you choose to save the page as source, you'll be able to view it any time you wish with Navigator without being connected to the Internet. To do this choose **Open File** from the **File** pull-down menu. You will then see a box

that prompts you to select the name and directory of the file you wish to open. Once the file is opened, it will appear exactly the same as it did when you originally saw it on the Web except the images from the page will be missing. Saving the page as text is done by following the same procedure as source. You can view a text file by opening it with your word processor. However, in this case, none of the original formatting of the page is preserved.

Images from Web pages are retrieved differently. To retrieve an image, move your mouse pointer over the image you want and hold the mouse button down until a window pops up. Then select **Save this Image as** and you'll be prompted to enter a file name and directory. The image will be saved in the *Graphics Interchange Format (GIF)*, which is a common 256-color format for Internet images. You may

ETHICAL USE OF INTERNET MATERIAL

Anything that you view with your Web browser can easily be copied and printed. For this reason, it's easy to overlook the fact that what you're copying was created by someone else. Authors probably won't object to you copying their Web page for your personal use. However, there's a good chance most won't be happy if you make multiple copies of their material for distribution to others without asking their permission—even if their page does not have a copyright notice. Sometimes authors encourage users to copy their materials provided their name appears on the copied document. Others strictly forbid copying unless written permission is obtained. You must obey the authors' wishes, otherwise you may be violating copyright laws. If there's nothing mentioned on a Web page about reproduction, always contact the author to request permission.

Options	Directory	Window	

General Preferences...
Mail and News Preferences...
Network Preferences...
Security Preferences...

✓ **Show Toolbar**
✓ **Show Location**
✓ **Show Directory Buttons**
 Show Java Console

✓ **Auto Load Images**

Document Encoding ▶

then view this image with any up-to-date graphics software package. Instead of selecting **Save this Image as** from the pop-up window, you could have selected **Copy this Image**. This stores a copy of the image in your computer's clipboard. You could then open your word processor and paste the image directly into a document.

Customizing Navigator

Once you gain confidence using Navigator, you'll want to look at the **Options** pull-down menu. Here you'll find menu items that allow you to alter the appearance of Navigator and

modify the way it works to suit your personal preferences.

Four items that you will likely want to select or de-select are: **Show Toolbar, Show Location, Show Directory Buttons,** and **Auto Load Images**. The first three of these are self-explanatory and allow you to have a larger window to view Web pages. This is especially handy if you're using Navigator on a notebook computer or a desktop computer with a small screen. The Auto Load Images requires an explanation. If you de-select it, the images that usually accompany a page won't appear when you access the page. In their place will be a small icon. When you click your mouse on the icon, the image will load. This is a very useful feature if you have a slow modem connection to the Internet because images take much more time than text to load. Some people use this feature like a television mute control so that

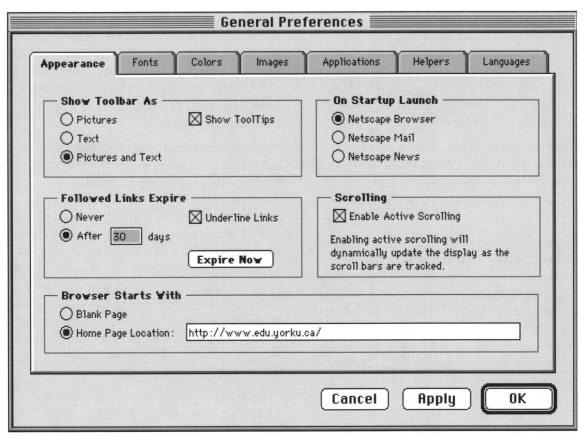

they don't see annoying ads on Web pages.

When you select **General Preferences** from the Options menu, you'll see tabs that allow you to set various features: Appearance, Fonts, Colors, Images, Applications, Helpers, Language.

There are two pages in General Preferences that we want to draw your attention to. One is the **Appearance** page. On the last line of the page is a space to enter the URL of the home page you'd like Navigator to open when you start up. Just above this line is a space to set the number of days after which links that you've looked at revert back to their original color.

Click on **Apply**, if you want the change to take place immediately, or **OK**, if you want it to occur next time you launch Navigator. The same procedure is used to set all preferences.

The other page in General Preferences you should note is the **Helpers** page. Helpers are separate software applications that assist Navigator in displaying files that it itself cannot handle, such as QuickTime video, Adobe Acrobat documents, and RealAudio sound files. This page tells you what helpers you have installed. You will know that you need a helper after Navigator gives you an error message when you're trying to view an image or listen to sound. A good collection of Helpers can be found at Navigator's home page (**http://www.netscape.com**), where they can be downloaded for free. Helpers come with instructions for installation and once these are followed, they appear on the Helpers page.

Beneath General Preferences on the Options menu is the **Mail and News Preferences**. We'll describe mail and news in the next two chapters and how to set up these preferences, so for now just take a quick look at them.

The final item we suggest you look at under the Options pull-down menu is **Network Preferences**. On the first page are the **Cache** settings. Navigator stores on your hard drive copies of the graphics and pages you look at in a folder (or directory) called the cache. When you click on the Back and Forward arrows or select a location from the Go list, Navigator will check the Cache first and load the local copy if it is there; otherwise it will load the page directly from the remote Web site. Caching speeds up browsing considerably because it's much quicker to load a page from your hard drive. You can adjust the cache size on this page, setting it anywhere between zero and the amount of space you have free on your hard drive. The default setting is five megabytes.

As you might expect, there could be a discrepancy between the copy of a page in your cache and the actual page if the page has been updated since you last looked at it. Navigator has two ways of dealing with this problem. First, you can click on the **Reload** button on the toolbar (or select it from the **View** menu) at any time if you suspect the page is not the most recent. This will always load the page from its original location. Second, on the Cache settings page you can tell Navigator how often it should check the original location for pages you've viewed by selecting one of the boxes: Every time, Once per session, or Never.

Protocols is the final page of the Network settings we suggest you look at. You should make sure the box for showing an alert before **Accepting a Cookie** is checked. Although the term "cookie" sounds harmless, it is something that all Web users should be aware of. A cookie is a file that resides on your hard disk containing information about your preferences for viewing specific Web sites. Its purpose is to allow a site to present you with a custom view based on your previous browsing habits at the site, something that can be a great convenience.

BOTHERED BY COOKIES?

You may find the cookie warning message annoying because it pops up often when you're browsing the Web. There's something permanent you can do to get rid of the problem if you don't want Web sites to know about you. You can delete the cookie file and replace it with a new folder or directory in the same location with the same name. Neither the Mac OS nor Windows will allow Navigator to create a cookie file if a folder or directory has the same name. You'll find the file, called **MagicCookie**, in the Netscape folder under Preferences in the Macintosh System folder. In Windows it's a file called **cookies.txt** found in the Netscape directory.

In order to store the information about you, the remote site must write information about you in the cookie file on your hard drive. When you return to the site, its server reads your cookie file so that it will know what view to present to you.

The fact that a remote site modifies a file on their hard drive upsets some people because they see this as an invasion of privacy. When you check the Accepting a Cookie box, Navigator warns you if a remote site is about to modify the cookie file, so you can then decide whether you want the site to modify it or not.

Key Concepts in This Chapter

- A full-featured Web browser, such as Navigator, is the only tool you really need for the learning highway.

- A URL is the Internet's equivalent of a ZIP or postal code and every Web resource has a unique URL.

- You can navigate the Web by clicking on hyperlinks, using the Back and Forward arrows, or accessing the History list from the Go pull-down menu.

- To go to a specific site, you can enter its URL in (1) the box presented when you click on the Open icon of the toolbar, (2) the Open Location box under the File pull-down menu, or (3) the Location line.

- Bookmarks provide a convenient way to return to a site without having to re-enter its URL. A bookmark is created by clicking on Add Bookmark under the Bookmarks pull-down menu.

- Web pages can be saved to your local hard drive, in text or source format, by selecting Save as under the File pull-down menu. Later you can view these pages without having to be connected to the Internet.

- The Options pull-down menu allows you to customize the appearance and other features of Navigator.

CHAPTER 6

How to Send Email with Netscape Mail

Electronic mail has long been the mainstay of the Internet. Each day millions of email messages are sent and received throughout the world. There is little wonder that email is so popular because it fulfills one of the most basic human needs—to communicate with others. The ability to communicate with so many people, whether they are around the corner or around the world, on any subject, and at any time, makes email the single-most valuable tool on the learning highway. For it is through interaction with others—expressing our ideas, reflecting, and responding—that we learn best.

Although version 3 of Netscape's email tool is not as full of features as others, or as popular, it is a good basic tool for learning how to use email. If your Internet service provider supplies you with another tool, such as Eudora, you'll find Navigator's email functions are very similar. In fact, you could use Navigator's mail in place of Eudora or any other package provided your mail is handled by what's called a **POP** (**Post Office Protocol**) server to avoid having to use a separate software application.

In this chapter, we'll describe the four main tasks involved in working with email: setting your mail preferences, sending mail, retrieving mail, and managing it.

Setting Your Email Preferences

To be able to send and receive email, Netscape Mail must connect to a POP mail server. This is a computer either in your school or at your Internet service provider that plays a role similar to the regular post office. You must connect to the post office to see if there is any mail waiting for you, and if you want to send mail, you need to deliver it first to the post office, which will then take care of distributing it to the correct address. Therefore, you must first tell Navigator the address of your mail server. This address may have already been entered when your computer was set up. To check, go to the Options pull-down menu and select **Mail & News Preferences**. Select the tab for Servers. Your school's or Internet service provider's server URL should be listed in **Incoming Mail Server** and **Outgoing Mail Server**. In addition, your email name should be entered in the space marked **POP user ID**. If any of these spaces are blank or incorrectly entered, you will not be

```
┌─────────────────── Mail & News Preferences ───────────────────┐
│                                                               │
│  ┌─Appearance─┬─Composition─┬─Servers─┬─Identity─┬─Organization─┐  │
│                                                               │
│   ┌─ Mail ──────────────────────────────────────────────┐     │
│   │   Outgoing Mail (SMTP) Server : │mail.utexas.edu    │     │
│   │   Incoming Mail (POP) Server : │mail.utexas.edu     │     │
│   │            POP user ID : │rdo                        │     │
│   │   Mail Directory : Macintosh HD :System ...ces :Netscape ƒ :Mail │ Browse... │ │
│   │   Maximum Message Size : ● None  ○ 40K ⇅ (Extra lines are left on the server) │
│   │   Messages are copied from the server to local disk, then: │
│   │        ● Removed from the server  ○ Left on the server │
│   │   Check for mail every : ● │2│ minutes  ○ Never        │
│   └──────────────────────────────────────────────────────┘     │
│   ┌─ News ──────────────────────────────────────────────┐     │
│   │   News (NNTP) Server : │newshost.cc.utexas.edu│       │
│   │        Get : │500│ Messages at a time. (Maximum 3500) │
│   └──────────────────────────────────────────────────────┘     │
│                          [ Cancel ]  [ Apply ]  [ OK ]         │
└───────────────────────────────────────────────────────────────┘
```

able to use Netscape for email. Check with your school network administrator or service provider to obtain the correct information to enter into these spaces if you are in doubt.

One other page needs to be set up too before you can begin. This is the page you see when you click on the **Identity** tab. In the blanks provided, fill in your name, your email address, and, if you want, the name of your school. There's also a blank for you to fill in a reply-to address. Most likely you'll want replies to your email to be sent to your regular email address, so enter it in this space too. On page 36 you can see the Identity page information illustrated.

We'll talk about the pages found on the other Mail preferences tabs as the need arises; for now you don't need to bother with them.

Sending Email Messages

FIRST STEPS

An attractive feature of POP mail is that you do not need to be connected to the Internet to compose your messages. You compose them off-line, and once they are all completed, you connect to the Internet and tell Netscape Mail to deliver them to the POP mail server. Your connection usually needs to be only brief for

Mail & News Preferences

| Appearance | Composition | Servers | **Identity** | Organization |

Identity

Your Name : Ron Owston

Your Email : rdo@mail.utexas.edu

Reply-to address : rdo@mail.utexas.edu

Organization : Dept. of Educational Administration, University o

Signature File

● None

○ File : [Browse...]

☐ Use Internet Configuration System

[Cancel] [Apply] [OK]

the messages to be delivered. Therefore, if you access the Internet via modem and pay an hourly rate, you spend considerably less money than you would if you had to use other mail systems that require you to be logged on to a remote server while you write your messages.

To prepare a message for sending, go to the Window pull-down menu and select **Netscape Mail**. You are then presented with a dialog box, shown on page 37, into which you need to enter your *mail password*. You should have received your password when you were given your email ID.

Once you click OK, you will see the Netscape Mail window. Note that the pull-down menu names along the top are similar, but not identical, to those of the Netscape Web browser. The same applies to the toolbar, which, again, provides a quick way to access the functions of the menus. As you see the screen is divided into three segments: the left is for handling messages you send; the right is for handling messages you receive; and the bottom is for viewing messages. There is also a status bar at the bottom of the screen that lets you know when Netscape Mail is performing a task.

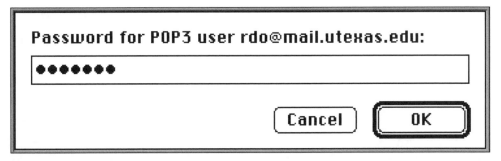

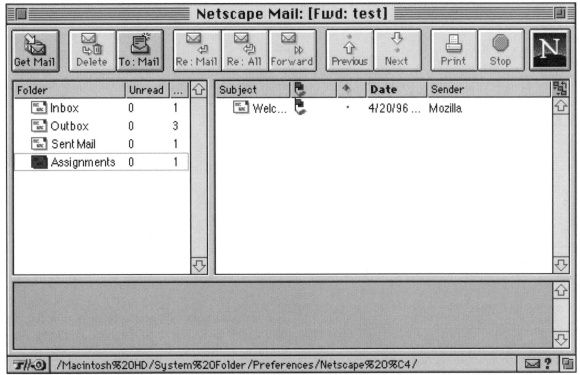

COMPOSING A MESSAGE

You are now ready to write your first message. To do this, click on the toolbar icon **To: Mail** (or select **New Mail Message** from the File pull-down menu) and you'll see the composition window illustrated on the next page. This window has three areas into which you can enter information.

At the top of the window is the **Subject** field. It's considered proper practice, something the Internet world calls *netiquette*, to include a message subject. This alerts recipients to the nature of a message, so they can decide which messages to read first; it also helps them retrieve your message later if they save it. Make the subject no more than a few words that

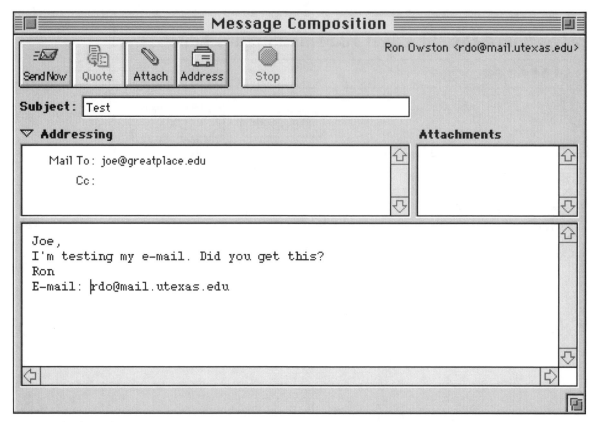

accurately describe the message's content.

Below the Subject field is the Addressing section, which contains the **Mail To:** and **Cc:** fields. You enter the recipient's Internet mail address in the Mail To field. If you want the message to go to more than one person, you can enter the other addresses one after another provided they are separated by a space or a comma. The Cc: field is intended for the addresses of people whom you wish to receive a copy of your message. Addresses are entered into the Cc: field the same way as they are entered into the Mail To field.

The large blank area in the window is for com-

posing your message. There is no reasonable limit on how much text you can enter, but some email systems cut off any part of a message that is over 1,000 lines long or greater than a certain file size. The best way to send someone lengthier text, or for that matter, any other kind of data such as graphics or a spreadsheet, is to send them the data in a separate file "attached" to an email message. We'll deal with this topic shortly.

AFTER YOU FINISH COMPOSING
Once you've finished writing your message, you can either send it immediately or delay doing so if you have others to compose, and

ABOUT EMAIL ADDRESSES

Internet email addresses always have two components: a user name and a domain. These components are always connected by an "@" sign. For example, in the address

`jdoe@greatplace.edu`

"jdoe" is the user name of the person you are sending a message to, and "greatplace.edu" is the domain. Sometimes you will see a user name made up of a person's first and last name separated by a "_" (underscore) or a "." (period), as in "John_Doe" or "John.Doe." This is done because there is *never* a blank space in an address. Internet email addresses are *never* case-sensitive. However, people often write them with upper- and lower-case letters to make them more readable. When you address a message, you can use all lower-case letters if you find that more convenient to type.

BE CAUTIOUS WITH COPIES

Newcomers to email often become enamored with sending the same message to many people, even though most of the recipients have little interest in the topic. Avoid this temptation. If you don't, you will annoy people and they will start discarding your email without even reading it. (Some email packages have a "bozo" filter that automatically deletes messages from certain addresses.)

Think long and hard before adding names to the Mail To or Cc list. Ask yourself if the potential recipient really needs a copy of your message. If in doubt, it is best to include too few rather than too many recipients.

send all the messages together. Netscape Mail calls these sending options **Immediate Delivery** and **Deferred Delivery,** respectively. You select the delivery method from the Options pull-down menu in the Mail Composition window. If you connect to the Internet via a modem, you should choose Deferred Delivery even if you have only one message to send. On the other hand, if you have a direct high-speed Internet connection, it doesn't really matter which method you choose.

After you set the delivery method, click on the **SendNow** (or **SendLater**) icon or choose **Send Mail Now** (or **Send Mail Later**) from the File pull-down menu. The composition window will close and you will see the main mail window, which will be similar to the one on page 40. If you chose Immediate Delivery and are directly connected to the Internet, the message will have disappeared from your Outbox and have gone to your mail server for delivery—if not, your message will be placed in the **Outbox** folder on the left side of the mail window. By clicking once on the Outbox, all of the mail messages waiting to be delivered will be listed on the right side of the window. When you are ready to send all your messages, you must connect to the Internet (if you're not already connected), then select **Send Mail In Outbox** from the File pull-down menu and your mail will be delivered.

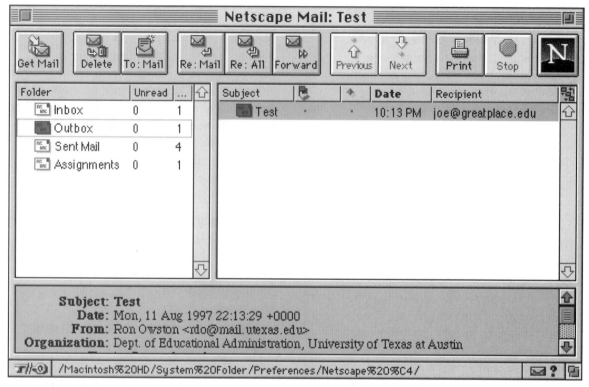

ATTACHING FILES TO MESSAGES

To attach a file to a message, click on the **Attach** icon on the toolbar (or select Attach under the File pull-down menu) of the message composition window. You will then see an **Attachments** box. Click on the **Attach File** button, locate the desired file on your hard drive, and click on Open. The file name will then appear in the window in the Attachments box. You can repeat this last step as many times as needed if you want to attach more files. When you've finished, click on Done. In the message composition window the name of the attached file will now appear and will accompany your message when you send it.

A word of caution about file attachments:

Don't assume that recipients of attached files will necessarily be able to read them. They must have the same software application and operating system that was used to create the file. For example, if you send a Macintosh Microsoft Word file to a friend who only has WordPerfect for Windows, he or she probably won't be able to read it.

Retrieving and Handling Email Messages

RETRIEVING MESSAGES

Assuming you are connected to the Internet, every time you open Netscape Mail it will automatically retrieve any messages waiting for you

THE BODY OF AN EMAIL MESSAGE

Email messages tend to be more casual than letters. Informality, however, is not an excuse for sloppiness. Common practice is to start the message with the recipient's name, usually omitting the salutation "Dear." The body of the message should be brief and to the point. A screen full of text is a good guideline for the maximum length. Never use all upper-case letters in your message BECAUSE THE INTERNET COMMUNITY CONSIDERS THIS EQUIVALENT TO SHOUTING AT SOMEONE.

You should always end the message with your name and email address. This information, together with a line or two containing your name and school, can be entered into a text file called a **Signature File**. Once you do this, you won't have to retype it every time you send a message. After you create the file, enter its name in the appropriate space on the Identity page of Mail and News preferences.

at your school's or Internet service provider's server. You can also retrieve mail at any time by clicking on the **Get Mail** button, selecting **Get New Mail** from the File menu, or clicking on the envelope-like mail icon at the bottom right of the browser window.

Netscape will automatically check to see if you have new mail at regular time intervals, which you can set on the Servers page of Mail and News preferences. When there is a message for you, the mail icon will have an exclamation mark beside it. Netscape, however, will not

KEEPING COPIES OF OUTGOING MESSAGES

To keep copies of the messages you send, check the box **Mail Messages: Self** on the Identity page of Mail and News preferences. Copies will then be kept in another mailbox called **Sent**, which will appear in the left pane of the mail window.

automatically retrieve this mail. You must take one of the previously mentioned actions to have it do this. To take advantage of this feature you need to be connected to the Internet.

Once your mail is retrieved, it will be stored in the **Inbox** folder in the left pane of the Mail window as shown on the next page.

WOULD YOU WANT YOUR MESSAGE ON THE EVENING NEWS?

A rule of thumb when you compose an email message is to ask yourself this question. If the answer is no, revise your message. It's very easy to dash off an impassioned message only to find later that you regretted it. Furthermore, Internet email cannot be considered confidential. The recipient can forward your message by the touch of a key to literally anyone— either intentionally or by accident. System administrators, too, typically have access to everyone's email on the servers they manage. They usually have better things to do than snoop, but a message may be incorrectly addressed, so they might look at it to try to determine its correct address. Always keep this question in mind before you hit the Send button.

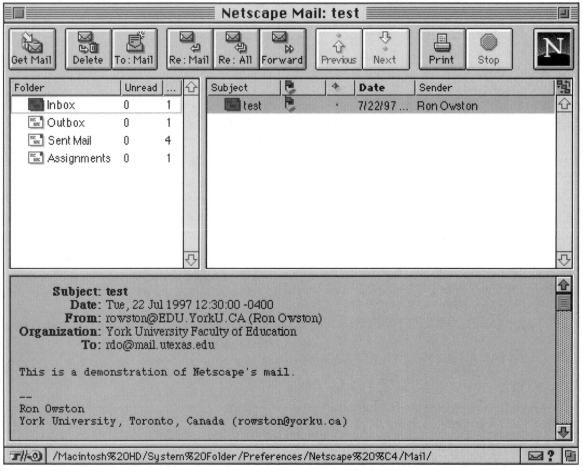

Immediately beside the Inbox are two numbers: the first tells how many unread messages the Inbox contains, the second indicates the total number of messages in the box. When you click on the Inbox icon, a list of messages appears in the right pane. For each message, from left to right, you see its subject, an icon telling you whether you've read it, the sender, and the time and date it was received. (You can change the order of these headings by dragging a heading with your mouse.) To read a message, you need only click once on the message and it will appear in the bottom window.

Occasionally you may want to flag a message for future reference or mark a message you've read as unread. This is done by selecting the message and choosing **Flag Message** or **Mark as Unread** from the Message pull-down menu.

REPLYING TO MESSAGES
You will obviously want to reply to many of the messages you receive. This is done by

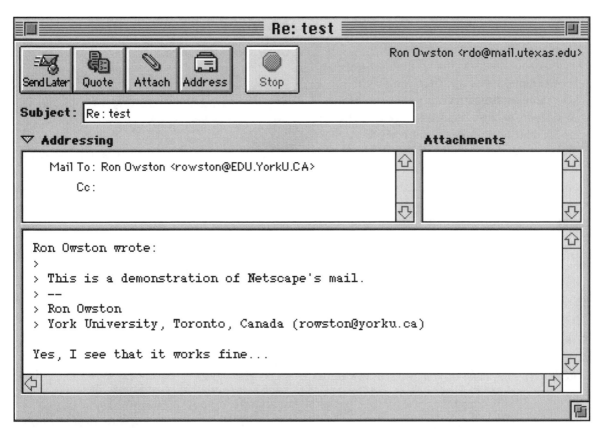

choosing from the list of messages the message you want to reply to and clicking on the **Re: Mail** icon on the toolbar (or **Reply** from the Message pull-down menu). A window to compose your reply will appear. If the **Automatically Quote Original Message When Replying** option was selected on the Composition page of Mail and News preferences, the original message will appear in the reply window. Each line of the original message will be preceded by a ">" mark. These marks indicate what the sender has said.

You can enter your reply anywhere in the window: before, after, or in between the quoted text. This allows you to respond to comments or questions posed by the sender without having to repeat or paraphrase them. You should delete any quoted text you do not want to use. However it is always good practice to leave a line or two of quoted text to remind the sender what he or she said in the original message. If you need to re-quote any text you've deleted, click on the **Quote** icon, which will cite the entire message again. After you're finished, click on the Send icon.

Notice the toolbar button **Re: All** just to the right of the Re: Mail button. Use this button when you want your reply to go not just to the

REPLYING TO DISTRIBUTION LISTS

Watch when you reply to a message that is sent to you as well as many other people—for example, a message that asks you if you are attending a meeting or event. This message may have originated from an electronic distribution list. If you reply to it, everyone on the list will get a copy. Since it's doubtful anyone other than the sender wants to know if you're going to the meeting, address your reply to the *sender's personal email* address, which most certainly appears somewhere in the body of the message.

sender, but to those who received copies of the message as well.

FORWARDING MESSAGES

From time to time you'll receive messages that you think will interest others and you'll want to send them a copy. You can also forward a message that you yourself have sent to someone else. To do this, select the message you want to forward and click on the **Forward** icon on the toolbar (or Forward from the Message pull-down menu). You won't actually see the original message in the composition window that appears. In the message space you may wish to type a note to the recipient such as "Thought this would be of interest...." When you're finished, click on Send and the message will be sent with your note on top followed by the original message.

Managing Your Email

DELETING MESSAGES

You'll be surprised at how quickly messages build up in your In, Out, and Sent mailboxes. Make sure to weed out messages you don't really need to keep from time to time, otherwise you will waste space on your hard disk. What's more it will be difficult to locate important messages among long lists of now insignificant messages. To get rid of a message from any mailbox, simply select it and click on the **Delete** button on the toolbar or **Delete Message** from the Edit pull-down menu.

ORGANIZING MESSAGES

If you're diligent about deleting unneeded messages, yet still find that you're accumulating quite a few, the time has come for your to develop a message organization scheme. Netscape Mail allows you to create as many additional mailboxes as required. Look over your lists of messages and think of several categories that they could be grouped into. You might categorize them according to the sender or the sender's organization, whether the messages are personal, job-, or school-related, or by the names of courses you are studying. The **Sort** command found under the **View** menu might facilitate this process since it allows you to re-arrange your messages by subject and sender.

Once you decide on the categories you want, go to the File menu and select **New Folder**. You'll be presented with a dialog box into which you enter the name of the new mailbox and click OK. The new mailbox will then appear under the others already there in the left pane. Repeat this step for all the categories you have. In any

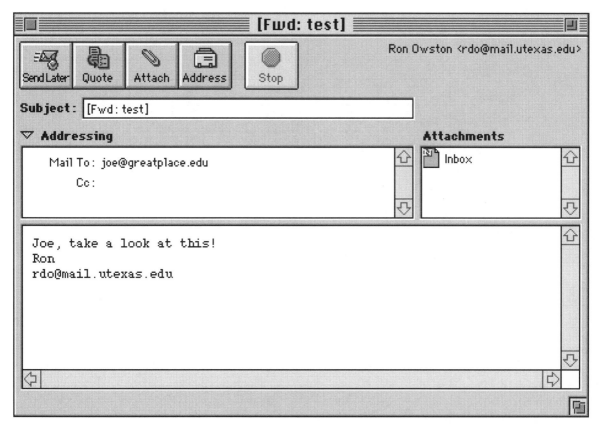

of the earlier screen shots that shows the left pane of the mail window, you can see that we have created a new mailbox called Assignments.

Next you are ready to file your messages into the new mailboxes. To do this, select from the right pane the message you want to move; then while holding your mouse down, drag it on top of the desired mailbox on the left and release the mouse. The message will be removed from the original mailbox and placed into the new one.

As you get into the habit of filing messages into the appropriate mailbox when you receive

them, you will find it much easier to locate old messages.

USING THE ADDRESS BOOK

Most of the time you'll find yourself sending messages to the same people over and over. It's a nuisance to have to type their full addresses each time you want to send them a message. Fortunately, Netscape Mail's **Address Book** eliminates this annoyance. Suppose you want to put the address of a friend, Sara Jones, into the book. First, select Address Book from the Window pull-down menu and the book will open. Next select **Add User** and a dialog box will appear (see next page) into which you

```
╔═══════════════════════════════════════════════════════════════╗
║                      untitled address                         ║
╠═══════════════════════════════════════════════════════════════╣
║                                                               ║
║      Nickname :  │Sara                                  │     ║
║                                                               ║
║          Name :  │Sara Jones                            │     ║
║                                                               ║
║        E-mail :  │sjones@heyu.ca                        │     ║
║                                                               ║
║   Description :  │Tel. 555-5555                         │     ║
║                  │                                      │     ║
║                  │                                      │     ║
║                  │                                      │     ║
║                  │                                      │     ║
║                                                               ║
║                                                               ║
║                              ┌──────────┐   ┌──────────┐      ║
║                              │  Cancel  │   │    OK    │      ║
║                              └──────────┘   └──────────┘      ║
╚═══════════════════════════════════════════════════════════════╝
```

enter your friend's name and email address on the appropriate lines. Note that there is also space called Nickname and Description. The nickname can be anything you want, for example, the person's first name, last name, or initials. (Don't worry, the recipient will never see the nickname.) We'll enter "Sara." The description space might be used to used to keep a record of the person's title, postal address, and phone number. When you're finished, click on OK.

Now suppose you want to send a message to Sara. You have two ways to take advantage of her name being in the Address Book:

1. Start a new message and enter Sara, her nickname, into the Mail To line. Click your mouse in the subject or message space and you'll see that her full email address will automatically replace her nickname on the Mail To line.

    or

2. Open the Address Book, double click on Sara's name, and a new message composition window will automatically open with her name already added in the Mail To line.

You are now ready to proceed composing and sending your message in the regular way.

Mailing Lists

Once you gain confidence using email you may want to try joining a *mailing list*, also called a *listserv*. A mailing list is basically a group of people with a common interest or affiliation who exchange email. A group of people who love the old Ford Edsel, for instance, may decide to form a list called **Edsel-L**, and welcome any other Edsel aficionados to join in their discussions. They begin by setting up a list of members' email addresses on a mailing list server. This server automatically distributes any messages it receives to all list members. New people who want to join the list send a subscription command to the server. Their names are then either added automatically or sent to the person responsible for the list for approval before being added.

More than 70,000 mailing lists exist on almost any topic you can imagine. Many of these lists allow anyone with an interest in their topic to join at no charge, while others are private. If you join a large and active list, you may receive dozens or more email messages a day; with others you may go weeks without getting any messages. All in all mailing lists are a great way to meet people and learn from talking to them.

There are several standard procedures for joining and removing your name from mailing lists, depending on the software that the mailing list server uses. In Chapter 10 we will show you how to locate lists on topics that may interest

SUBSCRIBE CAUTIOUSLY!
Remember to check your mail daily after you subscribe to a new mailing list because you probably don't have any idea how much mail the list generates. If it's an active list, your Inbox could easily be swamped in a day or two and you'll no longer be able to receive any new messages.

you with a service called Liszt. Once you identify a list, Liszt will provide you with exact instructions about how to join. Regardless of the procedure a particular list uses for joining and quitting, every list has two email addresses: the *list address* and the *administrative address*. It is essential that you understand the difference between them. The list address is the email address that you send messages to for distribution to others; the administrative address is the email address to which you send instructions for joining, quitting, and performing other tasks associated with your subscription to the list.

Key Concepts in This Chapter

- POP mail, the system used by Netscape Mail, is based on the concept of messages being delivered to and retrieved from a mail server.

- Email addresses consist of a user name and a domain name connected by an "@" sign. They are never case-sensitive, nor do they ever have a blank space.

- After you compose an email message you have the option of either sending it immediately or deferring delivery until you have completed all other messages.

- Any kind of file can be attached to an email message, but the recipient must have the software and operating system it was created in to be able to read it.

- While you are connected to the Internet, mail is retrieved automatically when

Netscape Mail is first opened. If it's already opened, when you click on the Get Mail button, select Get New Mail from the File menu, or click on the mail icon at the bottom right of the browser window to retrieve your mail.

- When you reply to messages, you have the choice of replying to only the sender (by clicking on Re: Mail) or to the sender and those who received copies (by clicking on Re: All). The sender's original message is quoted in the reply if the **Automatically Quote Original Message When Replying** option is selected on the Composition page of Mail and News preferences.

- The text of forwarded messages doesn't appear in the composition window; however, it is added automatically when the message is sent.

- It's good practice to delete unwanted messages and file your messages into additional mailboxes that you create.

- Names and addresses of people you frequently send messages to should be added to the Address Book to avoid having to enter them each time you send them a new message.

- Mailing lists are electronic distribution lists of people with common interests or affiliations.

CHAPTER 7

How to Participate in Newsgroups with Netscape News

Email is valuable when you want to communicate with specific individuals you know. But what if you have a question you'd like to pose to a wider audience? What if you want to meet other members of the Internet community who share your interests or have specific expertise? This is when you'll want to turn to *newsgroups*—the Internet's version of a community bulletin board. Newsgroups provide a forum in which you can discuss almost any topic imaginable (and some you can't even imagine!), find solutions to problems you have, help solve other people's problems, conduct research, gossip, rant, and rave. They've fallen in stature lately, the victim of the dramatic increase in use by newcomers unfamiliar with the norms of acceptable use, bad media coverage, and rampant commercialism despite restrictions on this kind of activity. Nevertheless, they are still an outstanding resource, well worth a stop on the learning highway.

This chapter begins with a short discussion of the basic concepts of newsgroups. We then describe how to use Netscape to read newsgroups and contribute to them. While the *Netscape News* tool is not as popular or as

intuitive to use as some news software, you'll find that if you understand how to use it you can apply the principles to any other news-reading software that you have.

Basic Newsgroup Concepts

To begin, you should be aware that there is a worldwide discussion system called *Usenet*. Usenet discussion groups are broadcast on a variety of different networks, of which the Internet is by far the largest. We mention this solely because some people refer to *Internet newsgroups* as *Usenet discussion groups*. This is perfectly correct. Others will use the terms *network news* or *net news*. They are also correct. It is important to understand that whichever of these three terms people use, they are all referring to the same thing. We'll use the term newsgroups or Internet newsgroups interchangeably throughout this book.

About 25,000 newsgroups exist, but not all of them are carried by all newsgroup servers. Typically, you'll see the following categories on larger news servers:

alt   A mixed bag of discussion ranging from topics that are bizarre and outrageous to the more serious

comp   Computer science and related topics

misc   A catchall for anything that doesn't fit elsewhere

sci   Scientific discussions other than computer science

soc   Groups that address a range of social and political issues

talk   Never-ending discussions of controversial topics

news   Network news discussions and announcements

rec   Discussions of the arts, hobbies, and recreational activities

In addition to these, you'll often find local area university groups and groups dealing with local city or regional topics, depending on where you live and where your Internet service provider or school gets its news distribution.

Newsgroups are arranged hierarchically by subject. All of the categories listed previously are top-level categories. For example, the category *sci* had 181 second-level groups at the time of writing, such as: *sci.aeronautics*, *sci.anthropology*, *sci.bio*, and *sci.virtualworlds*. Some of these second-level groups are further broken down into third-level groups. The group *sci.bio* has eighteen subgroups, four of which are: *sci.bio.botany*, *sci.bio.conservation*, *sci.bio.ecology*, and *sci.bio.etomology*. The latter group, *sci.bio.etomology*, has three more subgroups!

The advantage of the way newsgroups are organized is that it's relatively easy to locate a group that deals with a general topic that interests you. Suppose you wanted to find a group that discusses dogs. You'd go to the top-level category *rec;* inside that category you'd find *rec.pets;* and finally, you'd see *rec.pets.dogs* (which has subgroups about various breeds). It's a much greater challenge, however, if you want to find *all* groups that have discussed, say, "canine heartworm." This topic could be discussed in several of the subgroups of *rec.pets.dogs*, in some of the *alt* groups, and in various *sci* groups. In the next section, we'll talk about a research tool, DejaNews, that can help you tackle this kind of research problem.

When you contribute to a newsgroup, you are said to *post* an *article* or *message*. If you reply to an already existing article, you post a *follow-up article*. Some groups are *moderated*, which means a person in charge of the group has to approve all articles before they may appear. Within newsgroups, articles are arranged into

---

THE INFAMOUS ALT DISCUSSION GROUP
When the media and politicians talk about pornography, hate literature, and other inappropriate kinds of material on the Internet, they are often referring to some of the *alt* (*alternative*) newsgroups. While it's true that this category has more than its share of what most people would consider tasteless and offensive groups, when you take into consideration the total collection of newsgroup articles, this material makes up a relatively small proportion of their content.

clusters called *threads*. Threads consist of the original article and any follow-up articles. The advantage of threads is that you don't have to wade through hundreds of other articles to see the replies to a given article.

How to Read Newsgroups

CHECKING YOUR SETUP
Before you attempt to read the newsgroups, you should first go to the Servers page of Mail and News preferences to check if there's a URL entered on the line **News (NNTP) Server** (see picture on page 35). If the correct one is entered you're probably all set to begin; if not, you'll have to contact your system administrator or Internet service provider to get this information.

OPENING NETSCAPE NEWS
To begin, establish your connection to the Internet, start up Netscape Navigator, and choose Netscape News from the Window pull-down menu. You will see a window similar to the one below.

Netscape is preset to automatically send or "subscribe" you to two or three groups intended for new users from the *news* discussion group. The one we strongly recommend you first look at is *news.announce.newusers*. This moderated group contains a wealth of information explaining what newsgroups are, guidelines for acceptable use, and answers to frequently asked questions (FAQs) about newsgroups. In the illustration you can see in the left pane that we only received *news.newusers*.

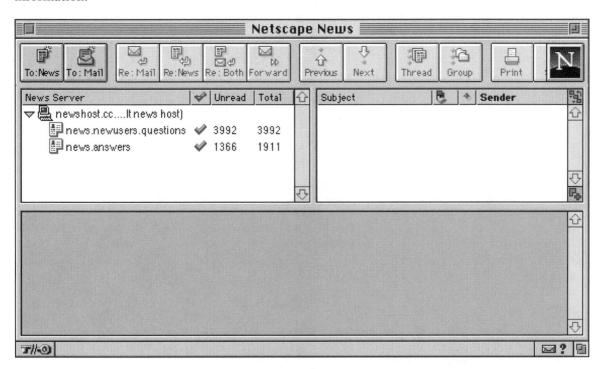

questions and *news.answers* when we started up Netscape. We'll show you how to subscribe to *news.announce.newusers* or any other news-group in a moment, but first we'll take a closer look at the three news window panes.

BECOME FAMILIAR WITH NEWS WINDOWS

As with the Netscape Mail window, you can resize the News windows, column widths, and re-arrange the column orders in any way you wish, so don't worry if your window doesn't appear the same as our illustrations. If you don't like the arrangement of the windows, you can experiment with the various options found on the Appearance page of Mail and News preferences.

By default the *group names appear in the left window* followed by a check mark indicating if you are subscribed to the group, the number of unread articles in the group, and the total number of articles in the group. You'll see beside some groups an indication in parentheses of how many subgroups can be found within that group. When you double-click on the group name (or click on the small triangle to the left of the group on the Macintosh) you can see its subgroups. This is illustrated in the picture below. The *right window contains the list of articles* for any group that you click on in the left window. From left to right in the article window is the subject of the article, a flag to

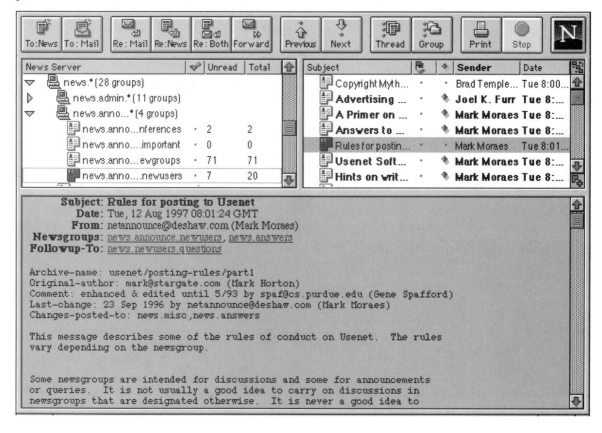

mark the article, an icon indicating whether or not you've read it, the sender, and the date. Note that if an article is posted the same day that you are reading it, a time of posting will be given but no date. To read an article, click on it once and the *article text will appear in the bottom window.* You can see that newsgroup articles look very much like email messages, except that instead of a "To" line there is a line marked "Newsgroups," which shows the groups the article was posted to.

BROWSING THE ARTICLES LIST

As soon as you click on an article to display it, the icon just to the left of the Sender changes indicating that you've read it. You can then move on to another article by clicking on its line or clicking on the **Previous** and **Next** buttons on the toolbar. At any time you can remove articles you've read from the list by selecting **Show Only Unread Messages** from the Options list. Some articles on the list are indented, which indicates that they are all part of the same thread.

As you browse through the list, you may wish to flag an article for follow-up reading by clicking below the flag icon. After you finish reading the articles you want in the group, you can return to the flagged articles by choosing **First, Next,** or **Previous Flagged** from the Go pull-down menu. Be careful because if you temporarily move to another group and return to the original group, you will lose the flags. You can keep any article you wish on your hard drive by clicking on Save As from the File pull-down menu and viewing it later with your word processor.

FINDING AN ARTICLE
Wading through a long list of articles in search of a particular topic or author can be tedious. Therefore, you may want to take advantage of Netscape News's **Find** command. This command, which is located under the Edit pull-down menu, allows you to search the article headers (i.e., subject, sender, date) of an entire newsgroup for any string of text.

After you've finished reading all the articles that interest you in a group, you can mark the entire group as read by clicking the **Group** button on the toolbar (or choosing **Mark Newsgroup Read** from the Message menu). Next time you return to the group you can then tell if any new messages have been added. Instead of marking the whole group as read, you can also mark individual threads as read so that you can check when new messages are added to it. This is done by clicking on the **Thread** button on the toolbar (or selecting

LIMITING THE NUMBER OF ARTICLES RETRIEVED
You may notice that Netscape Mail takes several minutes to load articles for very active groups. To reduce this waiting time, you can lower the number of articles retrieved at one time by reducing (from its default value of 500) the setting at the bottom of the Servers page of Mail and News preferences. When you want to see more articles, you can then select **Get More Messages** from the File pull-down menu.

Mark Thread Read from the Message pull-down menu).

Subscribing to Groups

There are so many newsgroups that it doesn't make sense to receive the entire set of groups carried by your news server each time you open your news-reading program. Therefore, Netscape News, like other programs, allows you to *subscribe* only to the groups that interest you. Subscribing to a group only means that you want Netscape Mail to send you the group each time you open it. Don't worry—there is no cost or commitment involved.

To see what groups you are currently subscribed to, select **Show Subscribed Groups** from the Options menu. Then to see what choices of groups you have to subscribe to, select from the same menu **Show All Newsgroups**. (There may be some delay before all the groups appear in the left window.) Let's say you want to subscribe to *news.announce.newusers*. Locate the group *news* from the list of groups in the left, double-click on it, locate *news.announce*, and then you'll see *news.announce.newusers*. Click in the subscribe column and a checkmark will appear. You are now subscribed to the group. To double-check, click on Show Subscribed Groups from the Options menu again and the group should appear along with the others you're already subscribed to. Repeat this process as many times as you wish to subscribe to the groups that interest you.

To unsubscribe to a group, just click again in the subscribe column and the checkmark will disappear. Note that the group name still appears in the list. You can refresh the list by

clicking on **Show Active Newsgroups** from the Options menu.

How to Post a Newsgroup Article

Posting a new or follow-up newsgroup article is very similar technically to sending and replying to email. The netiquette for posting and following up is more complex, so we recommend that you take the time to study our discussion. You are at your peril if you ignore this suggestion because newsgroup participants are notorious for retaliating against those who repeatedly violate accepted practices.

POSTING A NEW ARTICLE

For your first posting you should select a group that is specifically set up for testing. Look for a test group connected with your city or local university or any group that has a subgroup called *test*. We created the following test message for posting in the Austin, Texas, group called *austin.test*.

To create the message, simply click on the group you want to post to, then click on the **To: News** button on the toolbar or select New News Message from the File menu. Netscape's now familiar window for composing email will appear. The only difference is that instead of there being a line in which to indicate the recipient of the message, the name of the newsgroup will already be entered.

For a test message you don't have to worry about what you put in the Subject line; however, when posting a regular message give more thought to the Subject line than you would normally do for an email message. For example, if

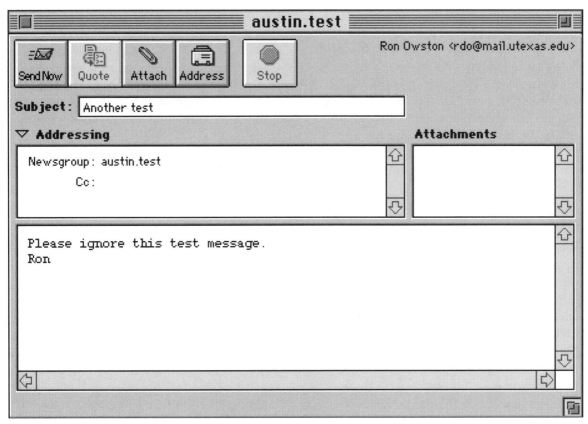

you wanted help creating Microsoft Word tables, don't just put "Help" in the subject line; put something like "MS Word Table Problems." Most newsgroup users scan messages looking for subjects that interest them, so the latter is more likely to attract someone to read your message.

After you enter your subject, you can proceed to compose a message and send it the same way as email. Don't be disappointed if your message doesn't appear in the newsgroup immediately; it could take as long as twenty-four hours for it to be posted.

SPAMMING AND FLAMING

Spamming is the practice of simultaneously posting the same material to many different newsgroups or email addresses. It is virulently opposed by the newsgroup community. Those who do this will most certainly be *flamed* by upset members; that is, they'll receive nasty messages condemning this action. Flaming isn't confined to just retaliation against spammers. Anyone who makes out-of-line comments or violates accepted practice in a group runs the risk of being flamed.

FOLLOWING UP ON AN ARTICLE

To follow up on an article, select the article you want in the right window and click on the **Re: News** button (or click on **Post Reply** from the Message menu). This time not only is the addressee of the message (i.e., the newsgroup name) already entered, but the subject is entered with the word "Re:" in front. You can then enter your reply and send it exactly the same way as you would with an email reply.

Note that there are two other Reply buttons on the toolbar: **Re: Mail** and **Re: Both**. Sometimes it's more appropriate to email a response directly to the author of an article rather than to the whole group; for example, when you simply want to say thank you to someone giving you help. This avoids having your message broad-cast to thousands of news servers worldwide, which in this case would be a waste of network resources. Click on Re: Mail to reply directly to the author. Other times, you may want your reply to go to both the group and the author, perhaps if you are unsure which the author will read first. The Re: Both button will handle this situation.

ACCEPTED PRACTICES FOR POSTING ARTICLES

New newsgroup users are often surprised to learn that, just as on the Internet itself, there is no central authority that controls newsgroups. They are regulated only by newsgroup partici-pants themselves. If enough users agree to con-duct themselves in a certain way, then that becomes the accepted practice. Some groups have their own specific norms. We do not have the space to delve into individual newsgroups; however, there are some widely accepted norms that apply to all groups. Below are a few of the key ones; if you follow these, you will be a wel-come member in any newsgroup.

- *Read Before Posting.* This is the cardinal rule of newsgroups. Never jump into a news-group; you must follow the group's discus-sion for a week or two before posting a message. See what kind of questions are asked, find out if threaded conversations are used extensively, what style of language is used (e.g., formal or informal), and who par-ticipates (e.g., senior researchers, students, the general public).

- *Research the Group in Advance.* Find out what is the general discussion theme of a group you're interested in before joining. Group names are sometimes misleading.

> ### WATCH THE REPLY ADDRESS!
>
> Some veteran newsgroup users are putting asterisks in their email addresses or alter-ing them in some other way in the set-up of their news software so that an incorrect address appears in the header of their mes-sages. (Note the bogus address of the sender of the message on page 93.) They then sign their name in the message body with their correct address. This is because they want to avoid commercial organiza-tions that rapidly scan newsgroup headers in particular groups in search of email addresses to add to "junk email" lists. These organizations rarely, if ever, look inside messages. Therefore, before you send off a reply to a message's author check that the correct address is in the addressee space.

Look for postings with the subject FAQ or subgroups whose name ends in *answers*. These postings often provide a good overview of the field of discussion and may answer questions you have about the group or its topic. You can access archives of newsgroup FAQs at **http://www.cs.ruu.nl/ cgi-bin/faqwais** or **http://www.lib.ox.ac.uk/ internet/news/**

- *Don't Advertise Unless You Know It's Permitted.* Commercial advertising in newsgroups is generally frowned upon, so to be safe don't do this unless you know that it is acceptable for a specific group. If you have something to sell, look for a group that is set up specially for advertising. Most cities, for example, have groups devoted to advertising local goods and services. These groups usually have names ending with *forsale*.

- *Limit Crossposting.* Posting a message to more than one group is known as crossposting. People do this to get a broad range of potential readers. Generally speaking, you should limit crosspostings to only a handful of groups. In fact, some people automatically ignore reading articles posted to more than two or three groups.

Key Concepts in This Chapter

- Newsgroups are the Internet's version of a community bulletin board.

- Newsgroups are organized hierarchically by subject.

- Although some 25,000 newsgroups exist, not all groups are carried by all servers.

- When you contribute to a newsgroup, you either *post* an article or *follow up* an article. An article and all its follow-up articles are called a *thread*.

- Posting or following up on an article with Netscape News is similar to creating a new email message, except that with a new posting the addressee is already filled in, and with follow-ups the subject is also already entered.

- After you choose Show All Newsgroups from the Options menu to see what groups are available, you may decide to "subscribe" to particular groups by clicking in the subscribe space to the right of the group name.

- To follow up on an article you have the choice of replying (1) to the group, (2) directly to the author, or (3) to both.

- Newsgroups have established proper usage practices that new users should respect.

LEARNING THROUGH RESEARCH

Introduction

By the time you finish reading this page another dozen or so Web sites will have been created, according to experts who monitor Internet growth. What's more, this rate of growth is expected to increase in the future. The World Wide Web is rapidly becoming an information utility unlike anything ever known to humankind.

Along with this explosive growth come greater opportunities for learning on the Internet. More and more material, such as government reports, encyclopedias, yearbooks, statistical reports, and scientific research, will only be published in an electronic format, accessed via the Web; background information, appendices, and follow-up material for printed texts, magazines, and newspapers are now available on the Web; noted authors, politicians, celebrities, and other public figures will be increasingly available for online interactive chat sessions with the public; "virtual communities" of individuals with common interests and concerns will continue to spring up in the form of mailing lists, newsgroups, and even three-dimensional Web-based chat rooms. The Internet will soon become the primary medium that allows educated persons to remain informed about their work, community, and the world around them.

Even though the Internet is becoming such a significant source of information, having access to it is no guarantee that you will learn from it, in the same way that simply having a library card does not necessarily make you a literate person. Access to the Internet will provide you with a powerful learning tool, but it is up to you to make the best use of that tool. The purpose of this section is to teach you basic research techniques and strategies that will help you use the Internet effectively in your studies, your work, and your daily life.

This section begins with an explanation of how to use the two basic kinds of research tools on the learning highway—Web directories and Web indexes. Known collectively as search engines, these tools are designed to help you locate information and resources as easily as possible. Next we turn to a discussion of how to search libraries and specialized databases. At this point, all major world libraries and databases containing indexes to publications are available online; therefore, it's essential for you to be adept at using them. In this discussion, we'll also show you how to search databases that contain newsgroup articles and software, as well as identify mailing lists of interest. We conclude the section by helping you put the skills you have learned together in order to develop a strategy that will allow you to thoroughly search the Internet for any topic and to evaluate your findings.

CHAPTER 8

Finding Resources with Web Directories

When doing research on the Internet you face a fundamental dilemma—resources are not cataloged or classified. Unlike libraries, which use a standard cataloging scheme such as the Dewey Decimal System or Library of Congress, Internet resources are simply "made available" to whoever happens to find them. Some Web sites, especially commercial ones, are heavily advertised, so you'll hear about them; but by and large you are on your own when trying to find out what's available. Even if there were a universal cataloging system, there would be no guarantee that everyone would use it or that resources would be accurately classified, because anyone can publish anything he or she wishes to on the Internet.

All is not lost, however, as innovative companies have stepped into the fray with tools that help people locate resources. Known as *search engines*, these tools focus primarily on locating Web resources because the Web is the segment of the Internet where most resources are now found. Though no single search engine will comprehensively search the Web, when you develop a strategy that combines several of these tools you will have left few stones unturned.

Two Kinds of Search Engines

Beginners—even some experienced Web surfers—often fail to recognize that there are two distinctly different kinds of search engines: directories and indexes. *Directories* are organized collections of links to Web resources. You can think of them as being somewhat like a book's table of contents. Links are usually added by human operators, who solicit Internet users to submit links and actively search for new links to add themselves. When you conduct a search of a Web directory, you usually look for keywords in subdirectory headings and in titles and descriptions of links to Web sites. The most comprehensive and well-known Web directory is Yahoo! In this chapter, we will explore this tool.

Web *indexes* consist of databases containing the full or partial text of sites. Continuing the book analogy, you may think of them as resembling the index at the back of a book. Their databases are built by automated tools called "bots," "crawlers," or "spiders," which roam the Web exploring links and collecting the entire content or abstracts of the content found

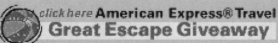

at those Web sites. When you search Web indexes, you search their entire database of text. As you might imagine, building a Web index is a herculean task requiring extremely powerful computers with massive storage capacities. Frequently, you'll find the companies that sponsor the popular indexes, such as Altavista, Hotbot, Lycos, and Infoseek, extolling the virtues of their search engines, claiming them to be the fastest and largest.

Competition among search engine companies to produce the best tool is intense. Many of the companies combine both indexes and directories at the same site. What drives the companies is the lucrative income gained by selling advertising space on their site and the possibility of selling the underlying search engine technology to other companies. Fortunately, consumers benefit from this competition as the tools continue to improve. The next chapter will explore

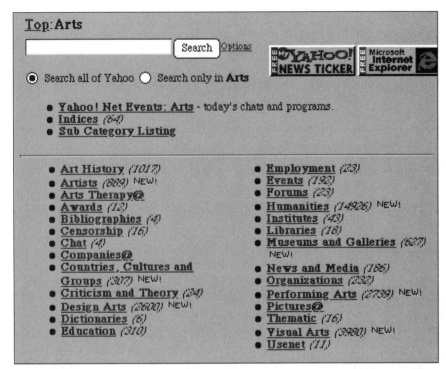

Altavista in depth—the Web index that we recommend because of its power, speed, and completeness.

Browsing Yahoo!

Yahoo! began humbly as two graduate students' list of favorite "hot links." So popular was the site that the students decided to make a go of it as a business. Today it has evolved into the premier Web directory, with specialty directories for major cities, countries, and children's resources.

Yahoo! is easy to use because you can just browse through its directory clicking on links until you find what you're looking for. You can also perform simple searches of the contents of the directory. To get to Yahoo, make sure you are connected to the Internet, launch your Web browser, and enter the URL

http://www.yahoo.com

into your Web browser or simply type "yahoo" (without the quotation marks). You will then see its home page. Because Yahoo!, like other search engines, is constantly updated, the page you see may not be identical to the one shown on page 62.

Yahoo! divides the content of the Internet into fourteen main categories, ranging from Arts and Humanities to Society and Culture. Underneath each main category heading is a sampling of the topics found in that category. For instance, under Arts and Humanities, some

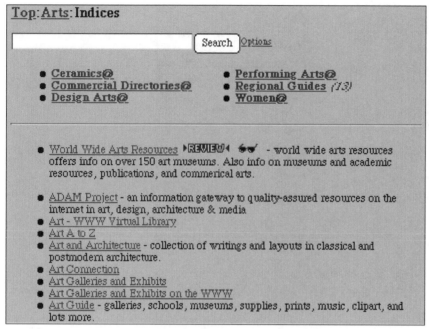

of the subcategories are Architecture, Photography, and Literature. You can click on any of these subheadings to be taken to lists of links and additional subcategories, but let's start at the top and click on Arts and Humanities (see page 63).

Toward the top of this page you'll see a search form, which we will talk about shortly. Below the form is the link Net Events, which provides a listing of links to various kinds of Internet chat sessions for the day. The next link, Indices, takes you to a page of links to directories created by others that are related to the Arts and Humanities. Shown above is a sampling of what you'll find on this page. These links are especially useful to explore, but you should realize that they are not part of Yahoo! The number in parentheses beside Indices tells you how many directory links are on that page. You will also notice an "@" sign beside some links. This is Yahoo's way of telling you that the link is actually from a main category other than Arts and Humanities, yet the link pertains to Arts and Humanities too.

The third item near the top, Sub Category Listing, takes you to a tree showing the hierarchical arrangement of all of the subcategories of Arts and Humanities. The tree, illustrated on page 65, helps you visualize how Yahoo! organizes its categories and subcategories. It also provides an alternative way of tracking down resources, as each category in the tree is a link that can be pursued.

When you return to Yahoo's home page, you may wish to browse some of the other links on this page. You'll find it fascinating, for example, to look at the city and foreign country Yahoo! home pages. You may also want to

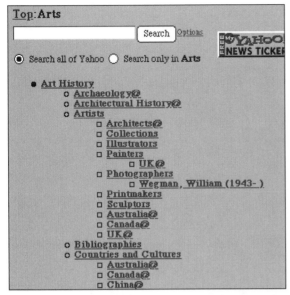

check out the links to news, weather, or sports scores, or the <u>Weekly Picks</u> link to some of the newest and best sites listed at Yahoo! Don't overlook the <u>Help</u> link, found at the bottom of all pages except the first, if you need more information about how to use the service.

Searching Yahoo!

On every page of Yahoo, you'll see a blank query box for conducting keyword searches. When you enter a word or words, Yahoo! searches for occurrences of the word(s) in its database of directory titles and the titles and descriptions of Web links. Yahoo! does *not* search the contents of the actual documents. In most cases, the link titles are very brief and sometimes provide little clue as to the contents of the document they link to. Also you'll quickly discover that not all links have descriptions, and when they do, they tend to be terse. This is a limitation of Yahoo! For example, the link in

the list of Indices shown on page 64 called <u>Art Connection</u> would be missed in a search on the topic of "art galleries," even though the site may be a rich resource of art galleries. This is because the site does not have the search words in its title and there is no description of the site available.

Now that you realize what Yahoo! actually searches, you can see that you are better off searching for general nouns or topics. For instance, search for "cattle" instead of "black angus cows," "Canadian history" rather than "Sir Wilfrid Laurier," "French artists" rather than "Monet," and "tropical diseases" instead of "malaria." Once you've located links to the general topic, you can then explore the links to see if any deal with your specific interest. We don't mean to suggest that you never search for

---

WATCH YOUR SPELLING!

When searching with Yahoo! or any other search engine, you should be aware of the differences between American and Canadian (or British) spellings. For example, a Canadian may be disappointed to find that a search for *child behaviour* produces very few hits. However, when the search is done using the American spelling, without the "u" in behavior, many more documents will be found. Likewise, an American searching for *autumn colors* may miss many splendid Canadian documents because the "u" is missing from colors. Therefore, to ensure that your search is thorough, make sure to search for both American and Canadian spelling variations of your keywords.

Found **96** Category and **601** Site Matches for **York University**.

Yahoo! Category Matches   [1 - 20 of 96]

Regional: U.S. States: New **York**: Cities: New **York** City: Education: Colleges and Universities: New **York University** (NYU)

Regional: U.S. States: New **York**: Cities: New **York** City: Education: Colleges and Universities: City **University** of New **York** (CUNY)

Regional: Countries: Canada: Provinces and Territories: Ontario: Counties and Regions: Greater Toronto Area (GTA): Metropolitan Toronto: North **York**: Education: Colleges and Universities: **York University**

Regional: Countries: United Kingdom: England: Counties and Districts: **York**: Education: Universities: **University** of **York**

Regional: U.S. States: New **York**: Education: Colleges and Universities: Public: State **University** of New **York** - SUNY

Regional: U.S. States: New **York**: Cities: Oneonta: Education: Colleges and Universities: State **University** of New **York** College at Oneonta

Regional: U.S. States: New **York**: Counties and Regions: Brooklyn: Education: Colleges and Universities: Polytechnic **University** of New **York**

specific nouns, because you could get lucky and find the exact word.

To carry out a search with Yahoo, simply enter the term or terms you have chosen in the query box and click on Search. By default Yahoo! assumes you want an "intelligent" search. This means that it will try to find items that contain all of your words, preferably with the words immediately beside or close to each other. The results of the search are presented in a list in order of *relevancy*, or the likelihood that the item is the one you want. Items containing your keywords are most often presented first. In addition, items that have the words in their title are presented ahead of those containing the words in their description, and matches found higher up in Yahoo's tree hierarchy (the more general categories) are ranked higher than those lower in the tree (the more specific categories).

Yahoo's intelligent search is by no means foolproof, so it's essential that you spend some time learning the finer points of its search capabilities. For example, when we did a search for York University, where we work, Yahoo! mainly turned up items related to New York City and New York University as shown above.

To avoid this problem, click on Options to the right of the query box. You'll then see the

LOOKING FOR SOMEONE?

Click on the People Search link at the top of Yahoo's home page, fill in the person's name, click on Search, and Yahoo! will search a database of phone numbers and email addresses. But don't count on a person replying to an email message—just because someone has an email address doesn't mean he or she uses it!

screen below, where you can specify how you want the search conducted.

Re-enter *York University*, click on the choice marked "An exact phrase match," then click on the Search button. You'll see that the results improve but remain dominated by New York.

We can still do better. Click on the link Advanced Search Syntax at the top of the page, where you'll be taken to a description of some of the special search language or syntax that Yahoo! uses. Here you'll see that entering a "+" or a "-" sign immediately before a keyword either requires that the word be in the results or not in the results, respectively. Therefore, if we enter *York University -new* in the query box and do a search on the exact phrase, we will be presented with links to York University only.

While we're looking at the advanced search

page, we should consider some of the other options. You'll see check boxes for "Matches on all words (AND)" and "Matches on any word (OR)." There's a significant distinction between these two options: the first finds only items containing *all* of your keywords, whether or not they are adjacent to each other; the second finds items containing one or more of your keywords. The remaining option for search methods, "A person's name," is slightly mis-

---

EXACT PHRASES

Another way to force Yahoo! to search for an exact phrase is to surround the phrase by quotation marks in the query box: for example, if you enter "York University" Yahoo! will look for the two words adjacent to each other.

Search Options | Help on Search | Advanced Search Syntax

`York University` [Search] help

◉ Yahoo!   ○ Usenet   ○ E-mail addresses

For **Yahoo!** search, please use the options below:

Select a search method:

○ Intelligent default
◉ An exact phrase match
○ Matches on all words (AND)
○ Matches on any word (OR)
○ A person's name

Select a search area:

◉ Yahoo Categories
○ Web Sites

Find only new listings added during the past [3 years]

After the first result page, display [20] matches per page

Please note that most of the options selected will not be carried over to other search engines.

Yahoo! Category Matches   **(1 - 2 of 2)**

Science: Space: Spacecraft: **Space Shuttle**

Regional: U.S. States: Maryland: Cities: Lanham: Business: Genesis Engineering Company - aerospace engineering firm specializing in transport containers for **space shuttle**/flight use. We are suppliers of many containers for the 1st and 2nd HST servicing missions.

Yahoo! Site Matches   **(1 - 18 of 74)**

Science: Space: Spacecraft: **Space Shuttle**: Missions: STS-78

- NASA Shuttle Web: STS-78 - flight of **Space Shuttle** Columbia on STS-78.

Science: Space: Spacecraft: **Space Shuttle**

- Usenet - sci.**space.shuttle**
- **Space Shuttle** Monitor - An auto-refreshing series of pages of current status, Nasa-TV, **space shuttle** current location, sighting opportunities, and more.
- Hot Topic: **Space Shuttle**
- **Space Shuttle** Models - several 3D model data sets for the shuttle
- **Space Shuttle** Overview - Flight hardware for the **Space Shuttle** is manufactured at many locations around the United States by NASA prime

---

leading because it simply searches for occurrences of your keywords that begin with upper-case letters.

One other choice on the advanced search page that needs explanation is the one that lets you select a "search area." These options control only how the results will be displayed—you get the same results regardless of which option you use. When you choose "Yahoo Categories," the relevant directory categories appear first followed by links to relevant Web sites. Note the results of the above search on the keywords *space shuttle* using this option.

The Web Sites option omits the listing of categories at the beginning and presents only the Web site links.

Once you become familiar with Yahoo's

options page and search syntax, you will realize how much better your search results are compared with simply entering keywords in the query box on the home page. Remember to check the Help link if you are unsure about how to search for a particular topic.

WHEN YAHOO! CAN'T FIND IT
When Yahoo! cannot find any occurrences of your keywords, it automatically sends them to Altavista to see if that tool can produce any hits. Unfortunately, your search syntax may not be carried over successfully, so you may want to redo the search in Altavista directly.

```
        Yahoo! Site Matches    (1 - 20 of 74)

Science: Space: Spacecraft: Space Shuttle: Missions: STS-78

   ●  NASA Shuttle Web: STS-78 - flight of Space Shuttle Columbia on STS-78.

Science: Space: Spacecraft: Space Shuttle

   ●  Usenet - sci.space.shuttle
   ●  Space Shuttle Monitor - An auto-refreshing series of pages of current status,
      Nasa-TV, space shuttle current location, sighting opportunities, and more.
   ●  Hot Topic: Space Shuttle
   ●  Space Shuttle Models - several 3D model data sets for the shuttle
   ●  Space Shuttle Overview - Flight hardware for the Space Shuttle is
      manufactured at many locations around the United States by NASA prime
      contractors and subcontractors.
   ●  Space Shuttle Clickable Map - currently, the clickable zones include the
      external tank, solid rocket boosters, space shuttle main engines, cargo bay,
      and crew compartments.
```

Combining Browsing and Searching

When you browse Yahoo's directory categories you will notice that there is a query box on every page. The query box gives you the option to search all of Yahoo! or only the category you're currently viewing. This provides a convenient method of restricting your search to a narrower field, a feature that is particularly useful when an entire search of Yahoo! produces too many results. For example, say you wanted to research the corporate culture of the Apple Computer company. A search on *Apple Computer* from the home page of Yahoo! would produce too many hits because the keywords would bring up links related to Apple computer hardware and software. You could refine the search, or alternatively you could click on the category Business and Economy and then restrict your search to this category. Often you will find that browsing categories and doing a search restricted to a particular category is an effective way to cope with the vast amount of information in Yahoo! on popular topics.

Using Yahoo! in Your Research

Now that you've seen how Yahoo! functions, let's use the tool to research a few topics.

EXAMPLE ONE

Say you have to write a research paper about the environmental effects of oil spills. Here's how you might proceed to research the topic.

1. Do a search on the general topic *oil spills*. At the time we did this, four category and forty-six Web site matches were found.

2. While these results are manageable to read, we will try restricting the search to *oil spills effects* to see if more pertinent sites exist. No category matches were found, but four site matches were retrieved, all of which dealt directly with the topic as you can see from the screen shot on page 70. (Note that the results would not be affected by "spills" or "effects" being in the plural form because Yahoo! looks for a keyword and its root.)

Found **0** Category and **4** Site Matches for **oil spills effects**.

Yahoo! Site Matches   (1 – 4 of 4)

Science: Biology: Marine Biology

- Research on Exxon Valdez **Oil** Spill - research papers on the **effects** of **oil spills** on shoreline ecology, marine life, birds, and archeological sites.

Society and Culture: Environment and Nature: Disasters: **Oil Spills**: Individual **Spills**

- Research on Exxon Valdez **Oil** Spill - research papers on the **effects** of **oil spills** on shoreline ecology, marine life, birds, and archeological sites.

Society and Culture: Environment and Nature: Organizations: Public Interest Groups

- International Tanker Owners Pollution Federation, Ltd. - detailed information about ITOPF and **oil spills** from tankers including historical data; fate and **effects**; clean-up techniques; planning and response; compensation; and sources of further information.

---

3. Read and make notes about the four sites. Save the pages to your hard drive or make them bookmarks.

4. Browse the categories in which these four sites are located (e.g., *Science: Biology: Marine Biology*) looking for other relevant sites.

5. Return to the results in the first step to explore the sites dealing with oil spills in general.

EXAMPLE TWO

Say you have to write an in-depth analysis of Shakespeare's play *Macbeth*. We suggest you follow this strategy:

1. See what a search on *Macbeth* will turn up. When we did this, the results were not promising because links related to the play are mixed up with other sites related to the surname Macbeth.

2. Search for *Shakespeare Macbeth*. When we did this, one category and three Web sites were found. All seemed relevant as you can see from the screen shot on page 71.

3. Read and make notes about the sites. When you examine one of these sites, you'll see that it has the complete text online, so you can save it to your hard drive, and then copy and paste quotations into your word processor when you write your paper.

4. Browse the category *Arts: Performing Arts: Theater: Plays: Playwrights: Shakespeare, William (1564–1616): Works* looking for any documents that might deal with Macbeth as part of a general discussion on Shakespeare's plays.

EXAMPLE THREE

Say you are a psychology or education student who has to write a paper about recent brain research that shows the importance of early stimulation on children's development. Here are some strategies you might follow.

1. Formulate some keyword search strings. For example, *brain research*, *child development*,

Found **1** Category and **3** Site Matches for **Shakespeare Macbeth**.

Yahoo! Category Matches   **(1 - 1 of 1)**

Arts: Performing Arts: Theater: Plays: Playwrights: **Shakespeare**, William (1564-1616): Works: **Macbeth**

Yahoo! Site Matches   **(1 - 3 of 3)**

Arts: Performing Arts: Theater: Plays: Playwrights: **Shakespeare**, William (1564-1616): Works: **Macbeth**

- Student study notes to **Macbeth**
- **Macbeth** In-depth - annotations, summaries, analysis, CD-ROM reviews, discussions, and links for the great play.

Arts: Performing Arts: Theater: Plays: Playwrights: **Shakespeare**, William (1564-1616): Works

- Falcon Education Link - offers a guide to **Macbeth** and links to valuable education sites for students and teachers.

child neurology, *child environment*, *child nurturing*, and various combinations of these may work.

2. When we tried *child development*, we got too many results. Therefore, we clicked on Options beside the query box and did a search requiring the exact phrase *child development*. This reduced the number of Web sites found from 240 to 47.

3. Add the keyword *research* to the phrase and redo the search, this time choosing the option "intelligent search."

4. Try other combinations of the keywords.

In the end, we found that step 3 produced the best results, although none were entirely satisfactory. When this happens, it's time to try using a Web index, such as Altavista, to search the actual contents of documents for the key

> **WANT TO ENHANCE YOUR REPORT WITH IMAGES?**
> At the top of Yahoo's home page click on the link More Yahoos, then look for the Image Surfer link under the heading *Other Yahoo! Guides*. Image Surfer lets you browse or search for images that you can download and use in a report or presentation. Before you use the image, make sure to find out if it has any copyright restrictions.

words. We will show you how to do this in the next chapter.

Other Web Directories

Although Yahoo! is an excellent Web directory, there are several others we recommend you look at too. They are:

- Excite (**http://www.excite.com**). This tool is one of the major Web indexes, but it also has a comprehensive directory that begins with fourteen top-level categories.

- Galaxy (**http://galaxy.tradewave.com**). A directory that has eleven major categories, which are divided into an extensive number of subcategories.

- Infoseek (**http://www.infoseek.com**). One of the popular Web search indexes; it also has a very complete directory of Web resources.

- Lycos (**http://www.lycos.com**). One of the earliest and most comprehensive Web indexes, which includes a directory to the "Top 5%" Web sites.

- Magellan (**http://magellan.mckinley.com**). A comprehensive directory that gives you the option of searching for Web sites that the company has evaluated.

Many more directories exist: some are good general directories to Web resources, while others are directories to specific fields. To find a listing of these look in Yahoo's category *Computers and Internet: Internet: World Wide Web: Searching the Web: Web Directories.*

Key Concepts in This Chapter

- The Web is growing at such an astonishing rate that it is destined to become the premier source of information for all human endeavors.

- Internet resources are not cataloged or classified; anyone can make all kinds of resources available.

- The tools for searching the Web are known as *search engines.* Two kinds exist, *indexes* and *directories.* Directories are analogous to the table of contents of a book; indexes, to a book's index.

- *Yahoo!* is one of the most comprehensive Web directories.

- To locate information in Yahoo, you can either browse its directory or do keyword searches.

- Keyword searches scan only directory category names, Web page names, and Web page descriptions—not actual Web documents.

- A good source to find links to other Web directories is in the Yahoo! category *Computers and Internet: Internet: World Wide Web: Searching the Web: Web Directories.*

CHAPTER 9

Finding Resources with Web Indexes

Indexes are extremely powerful tools for locating Web resources. On the surface they appear simple to use—enter a few keywords and, presto, the results come back. Many times when you do this you'll be lucky and find what you're looking for immediately at the top of the results list. However, when you don't locate what you want in the first few pages of results, skill is needed. This chapter will help you develop this essential research skill. For illustration purposes we are going to describe how to use Altavista, one of the most comprehensive and fastest Web indexes. You can apply what you learn about Altavista to other popular indexes, because most of them use similar search languages and display results in a similar way. We will mention some of these other indexes at the end of the chapter.

How Altavista Works

Altavista consists of three components: a Web spider, indexing software, and a query interface. The Web spider, affectionately called Scooter by the staff at Digital Corporation who developed Altavista, roams the Web collecting as many as six million Web pages per day. Scooter sends these pages back to the indexing software, which builds an index of every word of every page it receives. When a query is submitted to Altavista, the query software searches the index for the keywords and displays the results in order of relevance. The documents highest on the results list are those that contain the most frequent occurrences of the keywords.

Two query modes are available in Altavista: simple and advanced. You'll probably spend 90 percent of your time using the simple mode; however, it is valuable to understand how to do both types of searches. We'll begin by explaining how to conduct a simple search.

How to Do Simple Searches

After you start up Netscape Navigator and connect to the Internet, point your Web browser to Altavista's home page:

http://altavista.digital.com

and you will see a page similar to the following one on page 74.

To do a search, simply enter your word(s) in the query box on the home page and click on Search. Let's do this with the example of York

Search [the Web] for documents in [any language]

[   ]

[search] [refine]

Help . Preferences . New Search . Advanced Search

FREE DOWNLOAD: AltaVista Search Gets Personal!

Our Network | Add/Remove URL | Feedback | Help
Advertising Info | About AltaVista | Jobs | Text-Only

 **Digital Equipment Corporation**
Disclaimer | Privacy Statement
Copyright 1997 © All Rights Reserved

University from the last chapter and see what the results are like.

From the results page, part of which is shown on page 75, you can see at the top that when we searched for *York University* nearly five million documents were found containing these two words. Ten results are presented per page. For each result, you see a link containing the name of the page, a line or two describing the page, its exact URL, size in kilobytes (k), the date the page was created or last modified, and language. To get to any successive results page,

click on the appropriate button at the bottom of the page.

If you don't find what you need on the first few pages, try modifying your keywords to better describe your topic and redo the search. For instance, we could have added Toronto and Canada to the search string. You can also try using Altavista's Refine feature by clicking on the appropriate button in the query box. When we clicked on this button, we saw the box on page 76.

```
About 4560490 documents match your query.

1. York University: Mathematics and Statistics
     Welcome to the World Wide Web page for the department's information server. Departmental Information.
     Calendar of current events. Who is who in the...
     http://www.math.yorku.ca/ - size 3K - 5-May-97 - English

2. New York Site - West Side
     New York Site - Home Page - Detailed information about Manhattan's Upper West Side
     http://www.nyside.com/ - size 6K - 16-May-97 - English

3. Satterlee Stephens Burke & Burke LLP - New York & New Jersey Law Firm
     With a history spanning more than 100 years, Satterlee Stephens Burke & Burke LLP is a mid-sized law
     firm providing a comprehensive range of services..
     http://www.ssbb.com/ - size 4K - 5-May-97 - English

4. Mount Saint Mary College, Newburgh, New York
     Welcome to Mount Saint Mary College. ~ The College on the Hudson ~ This is the official. site of Mount
     Saint Mary College. Our beautiful 70-acre, hillside.
     http://www.msmc.edu/ - size 4K - 7-Apr-97 - English

5. The New York State Archives and Records Administration Home Page
     New York State Archives and Records Administration Home Page
     http://unix6.nysed.gov/ - size 4K - 19-May-97 - English

6. Penn State York
     Last updated on 27 FEB 97. This server is provided and maintained by the Penn State York C&IS
     Department. If you need to communicate with the keepers of...
     http://www.yk.psu.edu/ - size 701 bytes - 13-Mar-97 - English
```

In the box you'll see a list of topics that were found in the documents of the original search, with an indication, as a percentage, of how often the topics appeared in them. For each topic there is a pull-down menu of choices: Ignore (indicated by …), Require, and Exclude. You can choose one of these options for as many of the topics as you wish. When you're ready, click on the Search button to redo the query. In our example, we decided to exclude the first three topics because York University has nothing to do with the various cities and states listed; however, we did require that University be in the results. Our search brought us more pages related to York University, but we were not entirely satisfied with the results.

You are likely to discover that your success will vary considerably with the Refine feature depending upon the nature of the search topic. If you don't find what you want after several tries using Refine, you'll be better off doing a search with Altavista's query language.

Simple Searches with Query Language

Altavista's query language gives you control over how your keywords will be searched for in documents. In the York University example, Altavista looked for documents containing the two words *York* and *University* anywhere in the documents. Documents that contained the most occurrences of these words were presented first, followed by those containing either

Refine your search by requiring a few relevant topics,
excluding irrelevant ones, and ignoring the others.

GRAPH ▶

search *refine*

...	
Require	
✓ **Exclude**	20% **York**, new, state
Exclude	6% **Pennsylvania**, jersey, connecticut, massachusetts
Exclude	6% **Manhattan**, brooklyn, bronx, city, nyc, harlem, yorkers
Require	5% **University**, college, colleges
...	5% **Carolina**, vermont, hampshire
...	5% **Rhode**, dakota, mississippi, wyoming, nevada, nebraska, arkansas, montana, idaho
...	5% **Students**, school, education, teachers, educational, schools, classroom, curriculum, student

HOW COULD I EVER READ HALF A MILLION DOCUMENTS?

When you do an Altavista search on common words, don't be discouraged if more than half a million documents are found. If what you want isn't in the first few pages of results, it won't likely appear in the remaining ones. This is because all major search engines present the most "relevant" documents first. Generally speaking, this means the first documents are those that have the most occurrences of your keywords. Always retry your search with more precise keywords, rather than spending time reading too many pages from the original search.

DISPLAYING A PAGE WHILE SEARCHING

Beside the URL of each search result is a small page icon. If you click on this, Netscape will open another browser window so that you can read the contents of the page while keeping Altavista's search results accessible.

BOOKMARKING YOUR RESULTS

If you want to follow up on a set of results pages at another time, you don't have to re-enter the keywords. Altavista allows you to bookmark the results page so you can pick up quickly from where you left off.

word. But we really wanted documents containing the two words right beside each other. Here is the rule to follow:

- To force Altavista to search for words next to each other, surround the words with quotation marks.

When we enter "York University" in quotation marks we get much better results, as you can see below.

Note, however, that the list still contains references to New York. We can ask Altavista to exclude documents with the word *New* from the results list by following this rule:

- To force Altavista to exclude words from a search, place a minus sign (-) directly in front of the word.

On page 78 you can see that the results improve when we follow this rule by using the search string *"York University" -new*.

The converse of this rule also works if we want to make sure a word is included in the retrieved documents.

- To force Altavista to include words in a search, place a plus sign (+) directly in front of the word.

For example, there are two York Universities, one in Canada and one in England. So we could modify our search string to be: *"York University" -new +Canada* to make sure that the Canadian one is represented. (Another option would be to enter *-England*.)

Now that we have identified the university, we may wish to allow for the possibility that York University and Canada might appear in all lower-case letters in some documents. This spelling could arise because someone might

---

About 40012 documents match your query.

1. **York University: Mathematics and Statistics**
   Welcome to the World Wide Web page for the department's information server. Departmental Information. Calendar of current events. Who is who in the...
   http://www.math.yorku.ca/ - size 3K - 5-Mar-97 - English

2. **Welcome to New York University**
   Search NYU Web. New York University at a Glance. Welcome to NYU from President L. Jay Oliva. NYU Office of Public Affairs NYU Alumni NYU Information Center.
   http://www.nyu.edu/ - size 7K - 30-May-97 - English

3. **York University's Gopher/HTTP Server**
   York University's Gopher/HTTP Server. Please Note: York Gopher Development Frozen. About York University. Libraries. Telephone and E-mail Directories....
   http://gopher.yorku.ca:3394/ - size 648 bytes - 3-Apr-96 - English

4. **York University Libraries**
   YORKLINE Library Catalogue. [User's Guide] Periodical indexes & other databases. Electronic journals. Internet resources / Other libraries. Reference..
   http://www.library.yorku.ca/ - size 3K - 31-Mar-97 - English

5. **Faculty of Pure and Applied Science - York University**
   This page is maintained by the Faculty of Pure and Applied Science WWW Team. [webmaster@www.science.yorku.ca]
   http://www.sci.yorku.ca/ - size 3K - 30-Dec-96 - English

```
About 4751 documents match your query.
  1. York University: Mathematics and Statistics
       Welcome to the World Wide Web page for the department's information server. Departmental Information.
       Calendar of current events. Who is who in the...
       http://www.math.yorku.ca/ - size 3K - 5-May-97 - English
  2. York University's Gopher/HTTP Server
       York University's Gopher/HTTP Server. Please Note: York Gopher Development Frozen. About York
       University. Libraries. Telephone and E-mail Directories....
       http://gopher.yorku.ca:3334/ - size 849 bytes - 3-Apr-95 - English
  3. Faculty of Pure and Applied Science - York University
       This page is maintained by the Faculty of Pure and Applied Science WWW Team.
       (webmaster@www.science.yorku.ca)
       http://www.cus.yorku.ca/ - size 3K - 30-Dec-96 - English
  4. York University Overflight (Sept 30, 1993)
       York University Overflight (Sept 30, 1993) Sorry, but the detailed report does not yet exist. You can,
       however, view the CASI imagery. This mosaic has...
       http://www.eol.bts.ca/~freeman/York-U/york93.html - size 661 bytes - 31-May-97 - English
  5. York University Geophysics Group WWW Server
       Welcome to Space Geophysics at York University Department of Physics. This group is the base for the
       UK Sub-Auroral Magnetometer Network (SAMNET) and is...
       http://aurora.york.ac.uk/ - size 3K - 39-Nov-96 - English
```

make a typo or else spell the words that way intentionally. To be sure to capture all instances of the names, we need to follow another rule:

- If a word is entered in lower-case, Altavista will retrieve upper- and lower-case occurrences; however if a word is entered in upper-case, only that version will be found.

Therefore, our new search string becomes: *"york university" -new +canada*. There may well be other situations, however, where you want to make sure you retrieve only a proper noun (e.g., to find Turkey the country, not the fowl), so either way you can use the rule to your advantage.

Let's modify our search to illustrate one remaining feature of Altavista's search language that you can use from the simple query box. Suppose we want Altavista to find information about the various faculties at York University.

To ensure we find all pages that have either *faculty* or *faculties*, we should follow this rule.

- To broaden a search, place an asterisk (*) after the root of a word.

The asterisk is called a wildcard. So our final search string becomes: *"york university" -new +canada +facult**. The results of this search are shown above.

Advanced Searches

Altavista's advanced search feature allows you to perform the same kinds of queries as a simple search *and* allows you to control several other aspects of the search that may help you locate that hard-to-find document. To perform an advanced query, click on the Advanced Search link at the bottom right of the simple search query box. You will then see the query box on page 80:

About 63650 documents match your query.

1. **Faculty of Fine Arts at York University**
   The Faculty of Fine Arts at York University is one of the largest and most comprehensive programmes of its kind in Canada. All York Fine Arts programmes
   http://www.yorku.ca/faculty/finearts/home.htm - size 5K - 26-Mar-97 - English

2. **York Java Day 1996 Acknowledgements - Faculty of Pure & Applied Science, York**
   Welcome to JavaSci's Home Page. York Java Day 1996 - Acknowledgements. All of our presenters and panelists, plus all attendees. Sun Microsystems of Canada.
   http://java.science.yorku.ca/services/computing/javaday96/ack.html - size 1K - 28-Feb-96 - English

3. **York Java Day 1996 Logistics - Faculty of Pure & Applied Science, York Univers**
   York Java Day 1996. York Java Day 1996 - Logistics. This document presents logistics relating to York Java Day 1996. Introductory details and a schedule...
   http://java.science.yorku.ca/services/computing/javaday96/logistics.html - size 3K - 28-Feb-96 - English

4. **York Java Day 1996 Panel Session - Faculty of Pure & Applied Science, York Uni**
   York Java Day 1996. York Java Day 1996 - Panel Session. This document presents details relating to the Panel Session Discussion of York Java Day 1996....
   http://java.science.yorku.ca/services/computing/javaday96/panel.html - size 3K - 28-Feb-96 - English

5. **Faculty of Graduate Studies at York University**
   Faculty of Graduate Studies. Strike Update. Take a Tour of York! York Gazette on line! Programme Handbooks & FGS Calendar 1995-1997. Programme...
   http://www.yorku.ca/faculty/grads/grad/home.htm - size 8K - 29-Apr-97 - English

NATURAL LANGUAGE SEARCHING

The goal of most search engine developers is to make their tools intelligent enough to understand ordinary questions posed by users. This type of search is referred to as a natural language query. Altavista does a fair job of handling such queries, but it is far from perfect. Nevertheless, you can submit queries, such as, "What is the population of Peru?" or "How do I convert Fahrenheit temperatures to Celsius?" and get good results. Simply type your question in the query box—without the quotation marks—and click on Search.

In the main area of the box you enter your keywords connected by appropriate search language operators (the words or symbols that are used to join search terms). The operators permitted are AND, OR, NOT, and NEAR. It's not essential that you enter them in upper-case, but we recommend you do because it allows them to be distinguished from keywords. Also, you should not use the "+" and "-" operators in an advanced search because they are interpreted only as punctuation marks. You can, however, surround groups of words with quotation marks to keep them together and use the asterisk for a wildcard.

Here is the purpose of the four advanced operators:

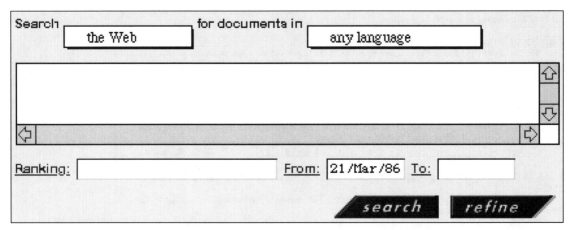

- The AND operator between two keywords tells Altavista to retrieve documents containing *both* words.

- The OR operator between two keywords tells Altavista to retrieve documents containing either *both words or just one of the two words.*

To give you an idea of the significant difference between the AND and OR operators, we entered the string *dog AND cat* in the advanced query form. After clicking on the Search button, Altavista retrieved 63,708 documents. The same search using *dog OR cat* yielded 695,065 documents—more than ten times as many!

- The NOT operator tells Altavista to exclude the word that follows it. For example, a search on *dog AND NOT cat* ensures that the word *cat* does not appear in any of the retrieved documents. The NOT operator is similar to the "-" operator in a simple search. Make sure to include AND before NOT because Altavista does not accept a search string such as *dog NOT cat.*

- The NEAR operator tells Altavista to retrieve documents that contain the two keywords *within ten words of each other*. For example, in our York University search, if we were looking for the Faculty of Education, a search using *Faculty NEAR Education* would allow for documents having *Faculty of Education* and *Education Faculty* to be retrieved.

When you do advanced searches with multiple operators, you should surround groups of search words with parentheses to avoid any ambiguity. For example, a search for *(Faculty NEAR Education) AND "York University"* ensures that only documents containing the words *Faculty* and *Education* within ten words of each other and *York University* are found.

Two other aspects of Altavista's advanced search features need to be explained: the *Ranking* field and the *From:/To:* field. The ranking field determines the order in which items will appear in the results list. In a simple search this order is determined automatically; however, in an advanced search you must complete this field unless you want the results listed in random order. The word or words you enter

---

WANT DOCUMENTS IN A FOREIGN
LANGUAGE?
In both Simple and Advanced searches,
you have the option of having Altavista
search for documents only in a specific
language. To do this, select the language
you want from the drop-down item in the
query box before clicking on the Search
button.

can be the same ones as your search words or
they can be entirely different. For instance, if
you entered *"York University"* in the query
box, you could put *Toronto* in the ranking field
so that out of the set of documents retrieved,
those containing Toronto would appear first.

Finally, you can specify a time period for documents by entering dates into the From:/To:
field. The dates must be in the form
dd/mmm/yy, where dd is the day of the month,
mmm is the name of the month shortened to
three letters, and yy is the last two digits of the
year (e.g., 08/aug/97). You do not need to specify a To date, which is a helpful feature because
you may wish to retrieve only documents created after a certain date. A word of caution is
needed because Altavista obtains the date of a
document from the document's Web server and
it may not always be accurate.

Using Altavista in Your Research

Let's return now to the three sample research
topics discussed in Chapter 8. We'll illustrate
how to formulate a search for them using
Altavista. We suggest you carry out the search-

es yourself so that you can make a first-hand
comparison of the differences between Yahoo!
and Altavista. In Chapter 11, we'll discuss
when it makes more sense to use one kind of
search engine instead of another.

EXAMPLE ONE

This example involves researching a paper
about the environmental effects of oil spills.
The best way to start is to do a simple search;
therefore we will enter *oil spill environment
effect* into Altavista's query box and click on
Search. We get the results list on page 82.

As you can see, 87,140 documents were
retrieved. All of those on the first few pages
seem relevant. This underscores a problem
you'll consistently face with Altavista and the
other Web indexes: namely, that they retrieve a
huge number of relevant documents. So at this
point you have to make a decision about focusing your research paper. You could limit your
paper geographically by dealing with the
Exxon Valdez oil spill in Alaska or with spills
in the North Sea. Another strategy might be to
look at the effects of spills on commercial fishing or on mammals. If you added some of these
terms to your search string, you'd undoubtedly
reduce the number of documents in the list and
make your project more manageable.

EXAMPLE TWO

This example involves writing an in-depth
analysis of Shakespeare's play *Macbeth*. Again,
it makes most sense to do a simple search. The
obvious keywords to use are *Shakespeare
Macbeth*. Page 83 shows a sample of the results
we got when we used them.

As you can see, an overwhelming 12,420 documents were found. A scanning of the list's first

About 87140 documents match your query.

1. Environment and North Cape Oil Spill
Environment and the North Cape Oil Spill. Late last year, our state's beautiful coastline was ravaged by the North Cape Oil Spill. The spill endangered...
http://www.ned96.org/textonl/environment.html - size 3K - 3-Jun-96 - English

2. Japan File Environment: Oil Spill
Useless black gold. The oil spill caused by the Russian tanker Nakhodka is the worst in Japan's history. Ed Gutierrez helped clean up. Our three chartered.
http://www.kto.co.jp/environment97_May_Useless_.html - size 8K - 26-May-97 - English

3. ENVIRONMENT: OIL SPILL DARKENS HORIZON FOR TOURISM AND SEALS
ENVIRONMENT: OIL SPILL DARKENS HORIZON FOR TOURISM AND SEALS.   By: Raul Ronzoni February 13, 1997, Thursday The world's largest reserve...
http://www.latinsynergy.org/oil_spill_uruguay.html - size 6K - 23-Jun-97

4. FishTalk '96: Re: WHAT EFFECT WILL THE OIL SPILL HAVE?
Re: WHAT EFFECT WILL THE OIL SPILL HAVE? GREG BELL (kjwaters@earthlink.net) Sun May 5 21:25:40 EDT 1996. I am a high school sophmore and I need pictures...
http://www.real-time.com/bbs/bbs30345.html - size 3K - 5-May-97 - English

few pages revealed that all the documents were relevant. Reading some of these documents might give you ideas about how to focus your paper. For example, several documents discuss whether the audience should have sympathy for Macbeth. To follow up on this topic, you could do another simple search using: *+Shakespeare +Macbeth +sympathy*. If you choose to do this, put a "+" sign in front of all three terms to force Altavista to return only documents that have all three terms in them. This will reduce the number of documents retrieved considerably. After reading a sampling, you may decide that audience sympathy is a good theme for your paper, or you may decide to look for a better theme by returning to the original list of documents and reading more of them.

EXAMPLE THREE
Our final example involves writing a paper about recent brain research that shows the importance of early stimulation on children's development. To conduct this search we will try using several strategies.

1. The best way to start is to do a simple search using the string of keywords: *brain research child development*. Most of the documents in the first few pages of results look promising, except that some discuss "brain child," which is off-topic. A partial view of the results is shown at the bottom of page 83.

2. To exclude "brain child" from the results list, we will conduct a simple search with: *brain research child development -"brain child"*. We get a much more relevant list, which is shown above.

3. Say you decide you now want to see only more recent documents. In this case, you do essentially the same search using the advanced mode instead. Note in the query box on page 84 that we enter 01/jan/97 for the date and ask for documents containing the word *child* to be listed first.

About 12420 documents match your query.

1. **Macbeth - Australian Shakespeare**
   THE AUSTRALIAN SHAKESPEARE COMPANY. presents. Shakespeare's. MACBETH. Directed by
   Neale Warrington. 5 Performances only ! Alexander Theatre Thursday 27 &..
   http://www.vicnet.net.au/~vss/macbeth.htm - size 1K - 27-Jun-96 - English

2. **Lambs' Tales From Shakespeare - Macbeth**
   Macbeth from Charles and Mary Lamb's Tales From Shakespeare.
   http://www.pubmar.edu/Library/lambstale/LTMACB.HTM - size 24K - 4-Jun-97 - English

3. **UWP Wisconsin Shakespeare Festival-Macbeth**
   Macbeth.   The Cast — The Story — The Stage History — Perspectives on Macbeth. Bloodthirsty Macbeth,
   urged by the prophecy of three...
   http://www.unpl.utt.edu/shakespeare/macbeth.html - size 3K - 26-Jul-96 - English

4. **Karaoke Shakespeare - Macbeth - $19 from CD-ROM Access**
   Karaoke Shakespeare - Macbeth. Karaoke Shakespeare/Macbeth - Animated Pixels - Jewel case - DOS - $19.
   Animated Pixels. Reference - literature. Ages:...
   http://www.cdaccess.com/html/pc/macbethk.htm - size 3K - 3-Feb-97 - English

5. **William Shakespeare. Macbeth.**
   William Shakespeare. Macbeth. (From the text of Clark and Wright.) 1. 1 W. When shall we three meet
   again. In thunder, lightning, or in rain? 2 W. When...
   http://m.irves.org/~vv/barth/tt00.htm - size 22K - 7-Jun-96 - English

---

About 516990 documents match your query.

1. **You Can Boost Your Child's Brain Power**
   The Sound Beginnings. Newsletter How to Develop Your Baby's Natural Gift for Languages Vol. 1, No. 1.
   You Can Boost Your Child's Brain Power. Intellectual.
   http://www.soundbeginnings.com/letter4.html - size 1K - 15-Jun-96 - English

2. **Brain Child**
   Brain Child. Now, in Brain Child, Turner has created an intense novel of muder and science that sounds the
   great themes of human identity and the nature...
   http://ezcall.lib.indiana.edu/~vvwin/authors/turner/brainchild.html - size 3K - 17-Feb-96 - English

3. **RESOURCE FOR BRAIN-INJURED Child**
   RESOURCE FOR BRAIN-INJURED Child. This article submitted by Chip Myers on 5/6/96. Author's
   Email: chipm@earthlink.net. I would highly suggest for anyone...
   http://lemon.mr.harvard.edu/newsweb/forum/MovementDisorders/Articles/RESOURCEFORBRAIN-In
   - size 3K - 26-May-97 - English

4. **Brain Child's Homepage**
   BRAIN CHILD. Welcome to James Weyhenmeyer II's Homepage. A Proud Student of The University of
   Illinois. MY LIFE. Links/Misc Spots. THIS PAGE IS STILL...
   http://pop.life.uiuc.edu/~weyhenme/ - size 3K - 23-Aug-96 - English

5. **BRAIN CHILD ELECTRONIC CO., LTD.**
   Welcome To. BRAIN CHILD ELECTRONIC CO., LTD. 6F, NO. 209, CHUNG YANG ROAD, NAN
   KANG DIST., TAIPIE , TAIWAN, R.O.C. 886-2-7861299. 886-2-7861395....
   http://www.asiapacific.com/taiwan/brain-child - size 3K - 11-May-97 - English

```
About 66230 documents match your query.

1. CHILD DEVELOPMENT
        CHILD DEVELOPMENT. Child Abuse and Neglect. 1965+ Available online, see Computer-Assisted
        Research Services (Ask at General Reference Desk — Level 3)....
        🗔 http://library.byu.edu/docs/pdt/1/chl_ind.html - size 3K - 8-Nov-96 - English

2. 51. Foundation for Child Development - Grants
        Prev | Top | Next ] 51. Foundation for Child Development - Grants. The Foundation for Child
        Development's grant making activities are focused on the...
        🗔 http://www.nyu.ed/tpt/r3/n11/tpt51.html - size 3K - 5-Jun-96 - English

3. Classic Theories of Child Development: The Theoreticians
        Child Development: The Theoreticians. Freud's was one of the earliest and most controversial of the
        theoretical developmental schemes. Margaret Mahler was.
        🗔 http://idealist.com/children/theory.html - size 913 bytes - 14-Apr-97 - English

4. Family and Child Development
        Family and Child Development. HE673-Principles of Parenting: The Challenge of Being a Parent.
        HE686-Principles of Parenting: Communication: Building a...
        🗔 http://www.essyr.auburn.edu:30/tp/publications/pub_asctii/HE/Fam_Chld.Dev - size 905 bytes -
        9-Jun-97 - English
```

Once again numerous documents were found. To narrow down the topic you could concentrate on the development of the brain during the first three years of life or on the importance of the parent's role in development.

Other Web Indexes

Altavista is an excellent "no-frills" search engine that we keep going back to time and again after using others. Nonetheless, we suggest you try out some of the other indexes, perhaps using the same keywords, to compare the results with Altavista's. For basic searches, all of the indexes allow keywords to be entered without any special syntax; however, when it comes to doing more complex searches, there are differences in syntax and procedures, so be sure to check each index's help page for details.

```
Search                  for documents in
        the Web                              any language

brain AND research AND child AND development AND NOT "brain
child"

Ranking: child                    From: 01/jan/97  To:

                                        search    refine
```

You can find a listing of indexes in Yahoo's category *Computers and Internet: Internet: World Wide Web: Searching the Web: Search Engines*. Below are some of the popular ones we suggest you look at.

- Excite (**http://www.excite.com**). A good comprehensive directory; however, we find that it tends to be slow, which will be a problem if your Internet access is via modem. For each document in the results list, Excite has a unique option that allows you to click on a link to find more documents like that one.

- Infoseek (**http://www.infoseek.com**). The results list is very similar to Altavista's; however, it has an added feature that suggests categories in its directory to browse to find more documents about your topic.

- Lycos (**http://www.lycos.com**). Provides an optional detailed description of the search results, which includes the number of words matched, an abstract, and a description of the resource.

- Hotbot (**http://www.hotbot.com**). One of our favorites—Hotbot is speedy, comprehensive, and has an easy-to-use interface. Handy options are available for locating various media types (e.g., images, audio, video), page types (e.g., front page, index page), location (e.g., continent, domain), and document date.

- Open Text (**http://index.opentext.net**). A good all-round search engine. Unlike Altavista, the results list provides a relevance score and its descriptions are slightly longer.

- MetaCrawler (**http://www.metacrawler. com**). This search engine does not have a database of its own. Instead, it submits search terms to most of the major search engines we've discussed and returns the results of all of those engines. We recommend you try MetaCrawler if you are searching for rare terms. As good as MetaCrawler is, you'll find that the results it gives for a particular search engine sometimes differ from those you'd get if you used that engine directly.

Key Concepts in This Chapter

- Altavista, one of the premier Web indexes, uses a powerful spider that roams the Internet collecting as many as six million pages a day.

- Two search modes are available: simple and advanced.

- Simple searches can be done by entering a string of keywords or a natural language question. Operators are also available to force certain words to be excluded or included in a search, to keep words together, and to search for variations of the root of a word.

- Results of simple searches are presented in order of relevance; the most relevant document is the one that has the most occurrences of the keywords.

- Advanced searches require the use of any combination of the operators AND, OR, NOT, and NEAR. You may optionally specify a date range and a language for the search.

- When doing an advanced search, you must enter a keyword into the ranking field to tell Altavista which results to display first; otherwise the results will be presented in random order.

- Look in Yahoo's category *Computers and Internet: Internet: World Wide Web: Searching the Web: Search Engines* to find a listing of links to other search engines.

CHAPTER 10

Finding Resources with Other Tools

Like good encyclopedias, Web directories and indexes are excellent general research tools. There are times, however, when you'll be looking for special kinds of resources, such as software, statistical data, books available on a particular topic, what people have said online about an issue, or what has been published in periodicals about your research topic. Although directories and indexes can be used to locate these kinds of resources, there are other Web tools dedicated to cataloging and indexing one particular type of resource that you should know about too. Not only are the databases of these tools likely to be more complete, you will find them much easier to use to zero in on your topic quickly. In some cases, like indexes of library materials, they may be the only tools you can use to locate that particular resource.

We will give you an overview in this chapter of the main tools we recommend you consider for your research on the learning highway. Our discussion of these tools will not be as extensive as our discussion of directories and indexes, partly because of space limitations, but also because they are simpler to use and therefore don't require detailed explanations. The tools that

we'll discuss and their purposes are:

TOOL	PURPOSE
Amazon.com	To locate books in print about almost any topic.
DejaNews	To help locate discussions about any topic in any newsgroup worldwide.
Liszt	To locate mailing lists (listservs) dealing with topics of interest.
SHAREWARE.COM	To locate software that is distributed freely on the Internet.
York University Library	To illustrate how to search a catalog of library holdings that are available to the public.

Finding Books in Print with Amazon.com

Amazon.com (**http://www.amazon.com**) is an online bookstore that has caused even the major national bookstores to take notice and set up shop on the Web too (e.g., Barnes and Noble, **http://www.barnesandnoble.com**). Its purpose is to sell books. We discuss Amazon.com here not to promote the company, but rather to illustrate how to use the store's remarkable database of more than 2.5 million books as a resource to help you research what print publications are available on a particular topic. Unfortunately, no library, not even the Library of Congress, has such an up-to-date database of the latest books in print. But don't worry, there's no charge or obligation to buy books when you search Amazon.com's database.

When you navigate to the site's home page, you'll see a banner running down the left side of the page that contains a menu of choices, including searching, purchasing a book, and reading book reviews and excerpts. This banner appears on all pages at Amazon.com. For locating books the menu gives you two choices,

searching and browsing by subject. The search options are: *author, title, or subject*; *keyword*; *ISBN*; and *advanced query*. We'll illustrate how to do a keyword search and briefly describe the other ways of searching as well as browsing.

KEYWORD SEARCHING

After you click on the <u>Keyword</u> search link, you'll see the now familiar query box shown below. Keyword queries are the most general form of searching at Amazon.com. You can enter any word(s), including authors' surnames (not first names) and titles, but note that the search engine restricts the results to books that contain *all* of the keywords you enter. This is the same as using the AND operator between all of the keywords in an Altavista advanced search. Words you want to keep together need to be surrounded by quotation marks ("..."), again as in Altavista. You also have the choice of searching for an exact keyword or using

---

<u>Home – Text Only</u>

SEARCH BY
<u>Author, Title, Subject</u>
<u>Keyword</u>
<u>ISBN</u>
<u>Advanced Query</u>

BROWSE BY
<u>All Subjects</u>
<u>Business</u>
<u>History</u>
<u>Science & Nature</u>
<u>Mystery & Thrillers</u>
<u>Children's Books</u>
<u>Religion</u>
<u>& Many More . . .</u>

BUY BOOKS

Search by Keyword

Enter one or more keywords. A keyword can be an author's *last* name, a word in a title, or a word in a book's subject category. If you use more than one keyword, the search engine will restrict the results to books that *and* match *all* the keywords you enter.

○ Exact Keyword(s)   ● Start(s) of Keyword(s)

> oil spill environment effect

[Search Now]   [Clear the Form]

Examples:

- Entering **"tolls whom"** finds Hemingway's *For Whom the Bell Tolls*.
- Entering **"bell hemingway"** also finds *For Whom the Bell Tolls*.

Note: Please do not use authors' *first* names as keywords -- they aren't included in our keyword index.

Four other ways to search the Amazon.com Catalog: by <u>Author, Title,</u> <u>and/or Subject</u>, <u>ISBN</u>, <u>Publication Date</u>, or <u>Advanced Query</u>.

Your Search Results
for: the keywords start "oil spill environment effect"

Eyes works while you play. Eyes sends you e-mail every time a new book is released in which the keywords start "oil spill environment effect". Sign up for Eyes!

---

9 items are shown below.

Marine Mammals and the Exxon Valdez ~ Ships in 2-3 days
Thomas R. Loughlin (Editor), Thomas R. Loughlon / Hardcover /
Published 1994
Our Price: $49.95
Read more about this title...

Exxon Valdez Oil Spill : Fate and Effects in Alaskan Waters (Stp, No 1219)
Peter G. Wells (Editor), et al / Hardcover / Published 1996
Our Price: $55.00 *(Special Order)*

Petroleum Effects in the Arctic Environment
F.R. Engelhardt (Editor) / Hardcover / Published 1985
Our Price: $141.50 *(Special Order)*

Aquatic toxicity from in-situ oil burning
(Hard to Find)

---

your keyword only as the root.

To illustrate a search, let's enter the keywords of the first search example we discussed in Chapters 8 and 9: oil spill environment effect. Then we'll click on the buttons Start(s) of Keyword(s) and Search Now.

The results come back in random order. All are relevant since each one contains all the keyword(s). When you click on a results link, you see detailed information about the book, including a summary, but remember it's not the book itself.

Some books have been reviewed by readers or magazines; links to them appear on the page as well. Also, toward the bottom of the page, you'll see an option that allows you to ask

Amazon.com to look for other similar books by subject.

OTHER KINDS OF SEARCHING

If instead of keyword search, you chose the link Author, Title, Subject, you'd be presented with a form to fill in the information you have about the book you wish to locate. You will usually get fewer hits if you do a subject search rather than a keyword search, because the field being searched is smaller.

Amazon.com's advanced query option uses a search language that is somewhat more powerful and complex than Altavista's advanced search language. For example, you could specify a search string such as: *subject is "oil spills" and published after 1990*, or *title starts (oil or pollution) and author is not Jones*. To get help

---

Marine Mammals and the Exxon Valdez
by <u>Thomas R. Loughlin</u> (Editor), <u>Thomas R. Loughlon</u>

Hardcover, 395 pages
Published by Academic Pr
Publication date: September 1994
Dimensions (in inches): 9.30 x 6.18 x .90
ISBN: 0124561608
List: $49.95 ~ Our Price: $49.95
Availability: This item usually ships within 2-3 days.

[Add it to your Shopping Cart]
(You can always remove it later...)

Browse other <u>Science & Nature</u> titles.

Reviews and Commentary for *Marine Mammals and the Exxon Valdez*

Have you read this book? <u>Write an online review</u> and share your thoughts with other readers.

Book News, Inc., 03/01/95:
Summarizes previously confidential US government data on the oil spill's effect on marine mammals, including sea lions, otters, seals, and whales, in Prince William Sound and the Gulf of Alaska. Appendices offer sample collection documentation and a list of other oil tanker accidents. Annotation copyright Book News, Inc. Portland, Or.

---

and to see some examples of how to make use of the search language, click on the link marked <u>Instructions and Some Examples</u>, which is found on the advanced query page.

The remaining search option, ISBN, allows you to locate a book by its unique identification number. This number, which is given to every book published, is normally found on the back cover above the bar code.

BROWSING AMAZON.COM

Browsing through Amazon.com's directory reminds you of Yahoo!; however, Amazon's directory is not as extensive. At the top of the browse list, some 25 subject links appear, each of which leads to one more subcategory. Beneath each subcategory, you find a list of only the top fifty titles in demand for that sub-

category—not a directory of all books about that topic in the database. This is a good place to go if you wish to see what's popular on a topic; otherwise you'll probably want to stick to searching.

Researching Newsgroups with DejaNews

Although most of the Web directories and indexes claim to search newsgroups, we find that none of them can compete with DejaNews (**http://www.dejanews.com**). Its database, which is updated several times a day, contains the full text of almost all existing newsgroups, even obscure ones in Russia, for example. In fact, it is so up-to-date that if you post a test message in your local city or university news-

The Source for Internet Discussion Groups

Power Search Help ?

Search for:

`oil spill environment effect` [Find]

Keywords matched: ● All ○ Any
Database: ○ Current ● Old
6/18/97 to now 3/19/95 to 6/18/97

Number of matches: 25

Results format: Detailed

Sorted by: Score

group today, there's a good chance it will show up in DejaNews tomorrow. DejaNews even allows you to fully participate in newsgroups by posting and replying to messages. This is a real advantage if your local news server doesn't carry the group you want. We won't demonstrate this aspect, but we will illustrate how to use DejaNews to research topics of interest.

Like most search engines, DejaNews has two search modes, Quick and Power. The query box for the Quick mode appears when you connect to the site's home page. You can enter any keywords you wish into this box and click on the Find button to retrieve a list of newsgroup articles containing your keywords. If you don't put any operators between the keywords, DejaNews assumes you want it to retrieve only articles containing *all* of your keywords. When

you see your search results, you are given the option at the bottom of the page of extending the time period of your search from the last few weeks' worth of articles in the database, which is the default, to the entire database.

Although the Quick search mode is handy, we prefer to use DejaNews' Power search because it allows you to control how the search is conducted and how the results are displayed. To look at this mode, click on the Power Search link on the home page. We'll illustrate it by once again using the keywords *oil spill environment effect*. We will enter them into the Power search form and choose to search the Old database, to display the Detailed results format, and to accept the default values for the other options.

Power Search Results Help ?

Matches **1-25** of **27** for search: | oil spill environment effect | | Find |

Re: Rainforest hardwood floors
Newsgroup: **alt.building.environment**
Posted on 1997/04/13 by Hugh Easton <hugh@no.spam.thankyou>

Re: Freshwater West: appalling pollution
Newsgroup: **alt.surfing**
Posted on 1996/02/21 by tpfbear@rain.org (Tbear)

Re: Rainforest hardwood floors
Newsgroup: **alt.building.environment**
Posted on 1997/04/15 by Mark <byron@eunet.si>

Re: Freshwater West: appalling pollution
Newsgroup: **alt.surfing**
Posted on 1996/02/23 by tpfbear@rain.org (Tbear)

After clicking on Find, we get twenty-seven matches, several of which are displayed above. The top item is the subject line of the article that contains the keywords; following it is the newsgroup that it was posted in, the posting date, a link to see what other articles the author has posted on any topic to any newsgroup.

When we click on the link to the first article, we see the text of the newsgroup article itself, which is shown on page 93. Note the handy icons above the article subject line. The two left-hand ones allow you to navigate up and down the results list, and the middle one takes you back to the results list. The **View Thread** icon provides you with a list of links to all the articles about the same *subject* (i.e., rainforest hardwood floors). These articles may or may not contain the keywords. The rightmost icon

allows you to actually post a response to the article.

If you wanted to refine your search, you could go back to the Power search form and click on Help. This link will take you to a page explaining the powerful search language DejaNews has. Essentially the language allows you to do everything that you can do with Altavista, but in addition, it lets you restrict your search to the author, subject, newsgroup, and creation date fields.

FINDING A NEWSGROUP TO JOIN
We cannot end our brief discussion of DejaNews without mentioning one more of its attractive features—the Interest Finder. This feature helps you identify newsgroups that will match your interests. When you click on the Interest Finder link on the home page, you will

Previous Article   Next Article   Current Results   View Thread   Post Message

```
Subject:     Re: Rainforest hardwood floors
From:        Hugh Easton <hugh@no.spam.thankyou>
Date:        1997/04/13
Message-Id:  <860968019snz@daflight.demon.co.uk>
Newsgroups:  alt.building.environment,sci.environment,austin.gener
[More Headers]

In article <5hg6j2$em4@camel0.mindspring.com> not_really@here.com "Bert" write:

>
> Do the terms "Three Mile Island" and "Chernobyl" mean anything to you?
>
What were the environmental effects of these two disasters. From what I
understand, TMI had no effect on the environment at all and Chernobyl
killed a few trees immediately downwind of the plant. Compare that to
the effects of a leaking oil pipeline or a tanker spill. Or acid rain.
Fossil fuels definitely harm the environment far more than nuclear does,
even without taking global warming into account.
```

see a query box into which you can enter keywords. After you click on Find, you'll see a list of newsgroups that have discussions about your topic; beside each newsgroup name is a confidence level, expressed as a percentage, that the group does, in fact, talk about your topic. When you click on any newsgroup link from the results list, you'll find a list of articles about your topic from that group. If you're overwhelmed by the sheer number of newsgroups, and uncertain about which one to "jump into," make sure to look at this feature.

Locating Mailing Lists with Liszt

Mailing lists are an outstanding way to do research through active participation. Some experienced Internet users prefer them to newsgroups because there's usually less likelihood of off-topic discussion and interference from participants who are not committed to the group. Often a major challenge with mailing lists, however, is to find out what lists are actually available to join. That's when Liszt (**http://www.liszt.com**) becomes extremely helpful. Liszt is a mailing list spider that queries servers around the world and compiles the results into a searchable database. Operators

```
      Search Liszt's main
I.    directory              environment                          go   [help]
      of 71,618 mailing      Junk Filtering:  ○ none  ◉ some  ○ lots
      lists:
```

also add lists that they discover or are recommended to them. At the time of writing, Liszt's database had more than 71,000 lists cataloged.

Liszt is easy to use. At its home page, you'll see two options for locating mailing lists: *search* and *browse*. To do a search, enter your keywords in the query box (illustrated above) and click on the Go button. If you don't get the results you want, you have several alternatives. Try redoing the search after changing the setting for Junk Filtering from the default position of **some**. This setting filters extraneous groups from your results list. **None** will give you fewer groups related to your topic; **lots** will give you more groups. Another tactic is to modify your keywords. Don't make them too specific or complex because Liszt only has fairly brief searchable descriptions of groups, much like Yahoo's descriptions. Note that Liszt does not search the *contents* of any discussion group— only its description. A third choice might be to use Liszt's rich search language, which is very similar to Altavista's. To find out more about the language, click on help beside the Go button. If you don't insert any operators between your keywords, Liszt assumes you want *all* words in the results list.

We searched the topic *environment* to see if we could find any groups we might join that talked about our example of the effects of oil spills. We didn't bother searching for *oil spills* because we assumed that no groups would be devoted to such a narrow topic. The results are presented in three parts. For each part, we've shown an excerpt of the results on page 95.

- Part I tells you which of the directories on Liszt's home page have subcategories dealing with the topic *environment*. These directories are not guides to all mailing lists in Liszt; rather they are directories to Liszt Select. This is a subset of the 71,000 plus mailing lists that permit subscriptions from the general public and are recommended by Liszt and its users.

- Part II gives the actual names of mailing lists from Liszt Select that deal with the environment and their descriptions. Although you can't see it from the screen snapshot, the list names are color-coded: green, which appears first, means Liszt has detailed information about the list; yellow means some information is available; red means Liszt requested information but hasn't received any; and white means Liszt either hasn't requested or hasn't received any details about the group. Each list name is a link to whatever information Liszt has about the group, including how to subscribe to it.

- Part III gives the names of lists (up to a maximum of 150) in the entire database that were retrieved by the keyword search. Many of these may be private lists, however. You can find out about this and other information by clicking on a list's name.

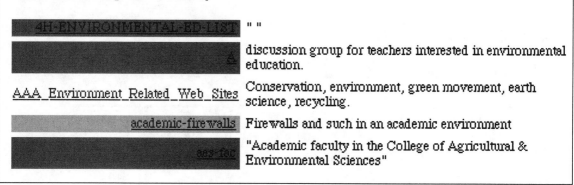

I. Your search on *environment* matched 4 Liszt Select categories:

Education/Environment (1 list) | Health/Environment (1 list) | Nature/Environment (12 lists) |
Politics/Environment (3 lists)

II. Your search matched 16 Liszt Select mailing lists:

arsenic — ARSENIC is an open discussion group of the health effects of arsenic in the environment.

CDROMLAN — CDROMLAN - USE OF CDROM PRODUCTS IN LAN ENVIRONMENTS

Committee for NATL INST for the ENVIRONMENT

STUDIES IN WOMEN AND ENVIRONMENT

ENVIRONMENT and GAME THEORY

ENVIRONMENT IN LATIN AMERICA NETWORK

III. Your search on *environment* matched 223 mailing lists (although Liszt will only show 150):

4H-ENVIRONMENTAL-ED-LIST — " "

A — discussion group for teachers interested in environmental education.

AAA_Environment_Related_Web_Sites — Conservation, environment, green movement, earth science, recycling.

academic-firewalls — Firewalls and such in an academic environment

aas-fac — "Academic faculty in the College of Agricultural & Environmental Sciences"

Now that you've learned how to do a search, let's return to the home page and look at the browse option for locating lists. You can see from the screen snapshot on page 96 that fifteen topics are available. You can follow any of the topic paths to locate information on lists related to the categories and subcategories given. As mentioned previously the lists in the directory are from Liszt Select, not its entire database.

LISZT'S MAILING LIST ARCHIVE
Liszt plans to archive the actual content of major mailing lists at its Web site. This will give you the option of researching what was said in

II. **...or click on any topic to browse *Liszt Select*.**

Arts (135 lists)
Literature, Television, Movies ...

Business (68 lists)
Finance, Jobs, Marketing ...

Computers (148 lists)
Internet, Database, Programming ...

Culture (134 lists)
Gay, Jewish, Parenting ...

Education (48 lists)
Distance Education, Academia, Internet ...

Health (123 lists)
Medicine, Allergy, Support ...

Humanities (188 lists)
Philosophy, History, Psychology ...

Music (141 lists)
Bands, Singer-Songwriters, Genres ...

Nature (69 lists)
Animals, Environment, Plants ...

News (26 lists)
International, Regional, Politics ...

Politics (70 lists)
Environment, Activism, Human Rights ...

Recreation (119 lists)
Games, Autos, Sports ...

Religion (66 lists)
Christian, Jewish, Women ...

Science (65 lists)
Biology, Astronomy, Chemistry ...

Social (19 lists)
Regional, Religion, Kids ...

SEARCH CATALOGUE BY

 Go Back   Help   Request   Home   EXIT

Library materials are described in indexed records in the online catalogue. Under the SEARCH CATALOGUE BY you can search for library materials using TITLE, AUTHOR, KEYWORD, SUBJECT, PERIODICAL TITLES, SERIES TITLE or CALL NUMBER.

 Title   Author   Keyword   Subject   Periodical Title   Series   Call Number

Choose one of the following actions:

- TITLE.
- AUTHOR.
- KEYWORD.
- SUBJECT.
- PERIODICAL TITLE.
- SERIES.
- CALL NUMBER.

CATALOGUE LOOKUP BY OTHER COMBINATION

[Go Back] [Help] [Request] [Home] [EXIT]

general:		,	AND
author:		,	AND
title:		,	AND
subject:	Shakespeare Macbeth	,	AND
series:		,	AND
periodical title:			

[Search Catalog] [Reset Query Values]

a list discussion and seeing what the conversations are like before joining. Be sure to look for this feature when you visit Liszt.

Searching Libraries and Specialized Databases

Libraries are an essential stop on the learning highway when you're doing research. Until fairly recently you had to travel to libraries to gain access to their resources. Now most major public and university libraries have become repositories of electronic information and services that can be accessed from any Internet connection. We'll use our library at York University (**http://library.yorku.ca**) to illustrate what resources are typically available at major libraries. You should pay an online visit to the library at your university or college, or if you're a high school student, your nearest public or university library, because very few school libraries can match the latter's resources. If you don't know the URL of the nearest library, call them or search Yahoo! Whichever major library you look at, if it can be accessed on the Web, it will resemble York's.

SEARCHING A LIBRARY CATALOG

When you navigate from York library's home page to the catalog of holdings, you are greeted by the search page, part of which appears on page 96.

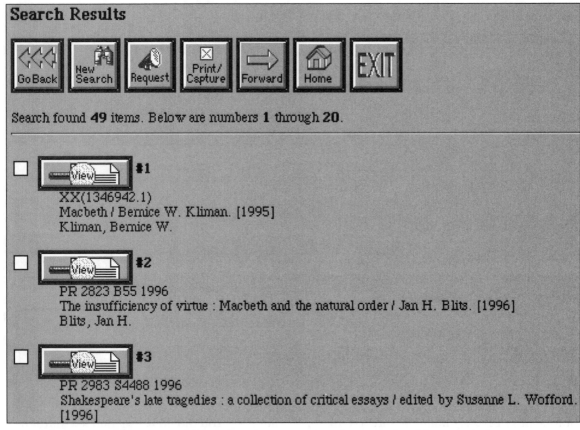

Search Results

[Go Back] [New Search] [Request] [Print/Capture] [Forward] [Home] [EXIT]

Search found **49** items. Below are numbers **1** through **20**.

☐ [View] #1
XX(1346942.1)
Macbeth / Bernice W. Kliman. [1995]
Kliman, Bernice W.

☐ [View] #2
PR 2823 B55 1996
The insufficiency of virtue : Macbeth and the natural order / Jan H. Blits. [1996]
Blits, Jan H.

☐ [View] #3
PR 2983 S4488 1996
Shakespeare's late tragedies : a collection of critical essays / edited by Susanne L. Wofford. [1996]

You may search according to: title, author, keyword, subject, periodical title, series, or call number. Keyword searches are the most general kind of query, so we'll demonstrate how to do one using the previous example that involved locating analyses of Shakespeare's *Macbeth*.

Clicking on the Keyword link or icon takes us to the search form shown at the top of page 97. We have to carefully consider which field we enter the keywords in. At first we might think that we should enter Shakespeare in the author field and Macbeth in the title field. That would be fine if we were looking for a copy of the actual play. But what we really want is to see what others have said about *Macbeth*.

Therefore, we should enter *Shakespeare Macbeth* in the subject field. We could also have entered it in the general field because that would cause all fields to be searched for the keywords. This would locate not only the plays themselves and what others have written about *Macbeth*, but many other items, too, such as authors with the surname Macbeth. We'd probably only do this if the subject field search failed to produce worthwhile results.

We entered the keywords and clicked on the button Search Catalog. The above screen shot shows three of the items on the results list that we got.

Search Result

Go Back — *New Search* — *Request* — *View Options* — *Print/Capture* — *Backwrd* — *Forward* — *Home* — *EXIT*

This is record number **2** of the **49** you found in the catalog.

☐ Check here to mark this record

PR 2823 B55 1996
The insufficiency of virtue : Macbeth and the natural order / Jan H. Blits.
Blits, Jan H.

Personal author:
  Blits, Jan H.
Title:
  The insufficiency of virtue : Macbeth and the natural order / Jan H. Blits.
Publication info:
  Lanham, Md. : Rowman & Littlefield, c1996.
Physical description:
  ix, 229 p.
Bibliography note:
  Includes bibliographical references (p. 203-222) and index.
ISBN:
  0847682501 (alk. paper)
ISBN:
  084768251X (pbk. : alk. paper)
Personal subject:
  Shakespeare, William, 1564-1616. Macbeth.
Personal subject:
  Macbeth, King of Scotland, 11th cent. In literature.

Clicking on any icon takes you to the catalog record for the particular item. The above screen shot shows what part of the record for the second item looks like.

Note that the record contains hyperlinks. They are helpful, for example, to find more works by the same author or to do a search for more on the same subject. As you browse records that look interesting, you can mark them by checking either the box just below the icon row on the record or on the results list. Then after you finish browsing, click on the **Print/Capture** icon and you'll be given a choice of either sending the results to an email address or downloading them.

WHY SEARCH A LIBRARY CATALOG?

As you saw in the previous example, a library's catalog gives you only bibliographic information about what is available on its shelves. This is helpful when you visit the library in person because you will know exactly what material to check out. But what if you can't get to the library—is searching the catalog still of any use? The answer is yes. If you are searching a remote library, you can usually arrange for an interlibrary loan of the material through your local library if your branch doesn't have it. Ask your librarian about this.

A catalog search also gives you clues that will help with online searches for Web resources. When you find library items that match your topic, you could try doing a search using Altavista to see if the same authors have published anything online related to your topic. More and more contemporary authors are publishing both in print and on the Web. Publishers are also putting excerpts of new books online. Therefore you could check to see if any of those found in the catalog are excerpted on the Web. The subject descriptors for items found in the catalog may provide additional clues for deciding what keywords you should use in an online search.

So make sure not to overlook library catalog searches as a way of tracking down Web resources!

OTHER ELECTRONIC LIBRARY RESOURCES

Beyond the catalog, many major libraries are teeming with online reference tools and the full text of articles, journals, and periodicals. For example, you might find searchable indexes such as the Applied Science & Technology Index, the ECONLit index for economics, ERIC resources for education, the General Science Index, the Humanities Index, the MLA index, PsycINFO, and the Social Sciences Index. These indexes are mainly used to locate print resources. In addition, libraries now have the full text of many journals online, including those published by Academic Press, the Expanded Academic ASAP, which contains more than 520 periodicals, and the Institute of Physics journals. The *Encyclopaedia Britannica* is found online at many libraries too. Unfortunately, access to these resources is usually restricted to those on campus because of commercial licensing agreements. Therefore if your campus doesn't have the materials you need, you won't be able to access them from another university. Make sure to explore your library to see what electronic resources are available and check with the librarian if you can't find what you want.

How to Find Software with SHAREWARE.COM

There's a vast amount of software available on the Internet that can be downloaded. If you know the exact name of the software you want, you can find a site from which to download it fairly easily with a search engine such as Altavista by doing a search using its name. But if you're looking for software to perform a certain task and don't know its name, the general search engines are not too helpful. For instance, suppose you wish to look for software for the Macintosh that will help you create Web pages. You could search for the keywords *html editors macintosh*, but you'd probably have to wade through numerous pages until you found a site that has this software to download. (HTML editors are what this kind of software is called,

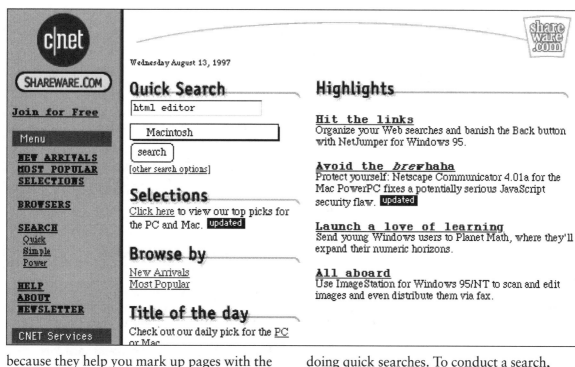

because they help you mark up pages with the HTML codes that browsers need to display the page properly.)

Fortunately, SHAREWARE.COM (**http://www.shareware.com**) makes the task of locating software easy. This outstanding site contains archives of thousands of different kinds of software for downloading: freeware, shareware, commercial software, and software patches. Much of this software is shareware, which the author expects you to pay for if you use it. Shareware is distinct from freeware, for which the author expects no payment. Always respect the agreement that you'll see on the screen when you launch shareware—even if you are a student.

When you navigate to the home page of SHAREWARE.COM, you find a form for

doing quick searches. To conduct a search, enter your keywords, choose the computer operating system that you use from the pull-down menu, and click on the Search button. Page 101 shows what you would enter to find a Macintosh HTML editor.

Page 102 shows a partial results list from the search.

When you click on a software title, you'll be linked to a page that presents a list of sites that have the software available for downloading, together with an indication of their reliability. Click on a site and you'll be ready to download the software.

Two more advanced search types are possible—simple and power. These allow greater control over how the search is conducted, but you won't

Search Results

File Platform: **Macintosh**
Description or file matches: **html editor**
Files per page: **25**

**Files from the cnet-mac archive
(since Aug 13,1997)**

Page_Spinner_2.0.sit.hqx
mac/internet/
Jun 03,1997
1592 K

Page Spinner 2.0 for the Macintosh, is a simple to use **HTML editor**. It offers point and click tag creation up to and including those in HTML version 3.2.

**Files from the info-mac archive
(since Aug 13,1997)**

new

html-grinder-321.hqx
text/html/
Jul 13,1997
1550 K

HTML Grinder Web site management software, the perfect complement to your **HTML editor**. 20 powerful Web tools: multi-file find and replace, check links, change filenames, build tables of contents, and lots more. Download the Grinder in Demo mode and keep the Find and Replace tool for FREE! Visit

need to use them unless you have very special requirements. If you want to browse for software to see what's interesting, you might check the links New Arrivals, Most Popular, and Selections. The last link is particularly interesting because it leads you to software, grouped by category, that SHAREWARE.COM recommends.

Key Concepts in This Chapter

- Many specialized tools exist that are more effective than general directories and indexes in locating particular kinds of resources.

- Amazon.com (**http://www.amazon.com**) has an extensive searchable database of books in print.

- DejaNews (**http://www.dejanews.com**) is an excellent, up-to-date archive of newsgroup articles.

- Liszt (**http://www.liszt.com**) will help you locate mailing lists dealing with almost any topic.

- The catalogs of major public and university libraries are on the Web. You can also search their other electronic resources, such as the full text of periodicals and special reference indexes.

- Software can be located by keyword and downloaded from SHAREWARE.COM's (**http://www.shareware.com**) vast archive.

CHAPTER 11

Research Strategies for the Learning Highway

The last three chapters helped you learn to do research with the major tools that are available on the learning highway. Now we'll look at how you can put your knowledge of these tools together to work for you. We'll explain some strategies you can follow to locate various kinds of information with these tools. These strategies won't be hard and fast rules, but rather some general steps you may wish to follow and modify according to your goals. Our discussion of strategies falls into three parts: finding facts, finding Web sites, and finding reading material. For each strategy, we've devised four steps to guide you through the process.

Merely finding information is not enough, however. You need to be able to assess whether what you find is worth using in your research. Therefore, after considering the three research strategies, we'll discuss how you can evaluate the quality of the information.

Four Steps to Finding Facts

Often you'll want to find specific facts, statistics, definitions, and other data. For instance, we might want to know the answer to questions such as:

- How high is Mount Everest?
- What is the GNP of France?
- What countries belong to the British Commonwealth?
- Who wrote the novel *The Sun Also Rises*?

Here are the steps we suggest you take to find answers to questions such as these.

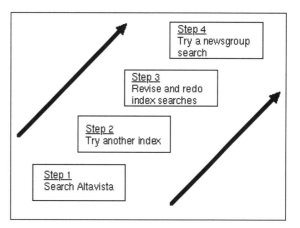

STEP 1

Think of the most obvious search words, paying particular attention to key nouns: for example, *height, elevation, Mount Everest* would be good for the first question above. Enter these words into a comprehensive search index, such as Altavista, and connect the keywords with appropriate search operators. For Altavista these might be +*(height or elevation)* +*"Mount Everest"*. Then do the search. If you don't find what you want, go to the next step.

STEP 2

Rather than refining your search with Altavista, try one or two Web search indexes because they typically produce remarkably different results with the same search words. You might even try MetaCrawler because it searches all of the major search engines in one step. Go to Step 3 if you still have no luck.

STEP 3

Your search skills will now be put to the test because you are going to have to go back and revise your search keywords and operators with the indexes and retry the searches. For example, we might try *(elevation OR height OR high) NEAR "Mount Everest"* in an advanced Altavista search.

STEP 4

If you're not successful in Step 3, then you should try searching the newsgroups with DejaNews. Given the vast amount of discussion that takes place in newsgroups, perhaps someone has previously talked about your topic. If you still draw a blank after searching DejaNews, then try posting a message in an appropriate group to see if anyone knows the answer to your question.

Four Steps to Finding Web Sites

This is a more open-ended kind of search than looking for facts, because if you're trying to locate Web sites that deal with a certain topic, you may never be satisfied that you've found them all. But more important than finding all the sites on a topic is locating good-quality sites that meet your needs. The steps we outline below will answer some of the following sample questions:

- What Web sites deal with modern English literature?

- Are there any sites dedicated to tornadoes—how they are formed and what safety precautions you can take if you see one?

- Are there any sites that have tutorials to help me improve my Spanish?

- Where can I go to find information on and see pictures of the Mir space station?

To answer questions like this, we suggest you follow the four steps described below.

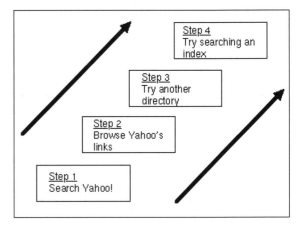

STEP 1

Yahoo! is a good starting point. Begin by either browsing your topic or doing a keyword search. For the last example about the Mir space station, browsing the path *Science: Space: Missions* would take you to a list of sites, as would searching on *Mir*. Since Yahoo! is an excellent resource for locating Web sites you may not need to look any farther, but if you do, try the next step.

STEP 2

Follow the path in Yahoo! to a subcategory that takes you closest to your topic and browse some of the links to sites that you find there. There's a good chance that a few of these sites will have links to your topic. But if you don't discover anything relevant, or conversely, if you find too many sites, go to Step 3.

STEP 3

Browse another directory. Magellan is a good one to try—pay particular attention to their evaluated sites. It's possible to browse only sites that are highly rated, for example. You may also want to browse the Top 5% sites at Lycos.

STEP 4

Try searching Altavista or any of the other major Web indexes if you still can't find what you want. We suggest using the indexes as a last resort for locating Web sites, because they often turn up too many links in their results list, especially when you are searching for a relatively broad topic.

Four Steps to Finding Reading Material

These steps will help you find articles, abstracts, essays, book excerpts, research papers, stories, poetry, and other kinds of original reading material. They are designed to help you locate suitable background reading for

your courses or special interests, and to find material for assignments or papers. By following these steps, you should be able to answer questions like:

- What has been written recently about the treatment of dyslexia in young children?

- Is there any research that suggests a connection between movie stars smoking on screen and teenage use of tobacco?

- Why was the U.S. involved in the Vietnam War?

- Why do some economists say that high unemployment can be "good" for the economy?

Below are the four steps we suggest you try.

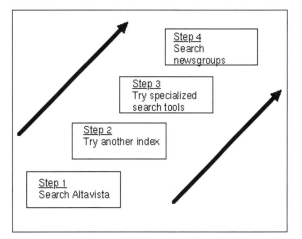

STEP 1

Try doing a search on your topic using Altavista. As a first step you may even want to enter a natural language question like any of the above and see how Altavista handles it. If that doesn't work, try entering keywords connected by appropriate operators. At this point don't spend too much time attempting to formulate a "perfect" search.

STEP 2

If Altavista doesn't locate what you want after a few tries, search a few other Web indexes or use MetaCrawler. Generally speaking, Yahoo! and the other Web directories are not as useful as the indexes for locating articles about specific topics, but there's no harm in giving them a go too.

STEP 3

Try some of the other specialized search tools if you still are not satisfied with what you've found so far. For example, search the catalog of your local library or that of a highly regarded university for your topic. Also try searching Amazon.com. The libraries and bookstores will likely point the way to relevant print materials you might be able to borrow or purchase; they may also suggest authors and keywords you can use for Steps 1 and 2.

STEP 4

Turn to DejaNews and search the newsgroups for your topic, if the first three steps prove

---

FINDING MAILING LISTS, NEWSGROUPS, AND SOFTWARE

We didn't include separate strategies for finding these three resources because each has a specialized tool to locate them, as discussed in Chapter 6. If you don't find what you want with these tools, then try searching Altavista or one of the other Web indexes. You could also check Yahoo! for links leading to other specialized search tools for these types of resources.

---

unproductive. You won't find actual reading material about your topic there, but you may come across someone who has discussed the topic and has referred to resources on the topic. If a Web site is mentioned in the body of a newsgroup article, DejaNews turns it into a clickable link that you could pursue with your browser. As a last resort, you could post a newsgroup message for help in an appropriate group.

Evaluating What You Find

With the traditional publishing of articles, books, magazines, and newspapers there is a built-in editorial process. Publishing houses employ editors to review manuscripts for content and style before they go to press. This process gives the reader some assurance that, at a minimum, someone else has read the material and deemed it worthy of publication. However, as we said earlier, on the Internet anyone can publish anything about any topic he or she wishes and can do so without having it scrutinized by an editor. Therefore, the caveat on the Internet is "Reader Beware!"

Besides looking out for erroneous information and reading critically, there are some other criteria you can use to evaluate what you read on the Internet. Here are some we recommend.

- *Look at the resource's domain name.* Domain names can provide some clues to the credibility of a resource. Generally speaking, we tend to trust documents that have domain names ending in *edu* or *gov*, because those names tell you that the documents come from a U.S. university or government site. If the site is outside the U.S., look for a university or government name as part of the domain name (e.g., *yorku.ca*). Commercial sites (*com*) of well-known, reputable companies are credible, too, but you must watch for biases that may relate to a company's product. For example, would you trust documents at a cigarette manufacturer's site about research linking smoking and cancer? Would these be as objective as a government report? Sites ending in *org* or *net* can be trusted if they are operated by a reputable organization too (e.g., the Public Broadcasting System, whose domain name is **http://www.pbs.org**), but watch for advocacy and special interest group sites because they may be presenting a specific slant on a topic to further their organization's goals.

- *Look for a document's author.* Never accept or quote from a document that is anonymous. We believe that anyone who publishes a document on the Internet would sign it if they think it's worthwhile. Once you identify the author, try to find out about his or her background. This may be as simple as clicking on a link on the document to the author's home page, or as bothersome as searching for an author's name with a Web index to see what you can unearth.

- *Try to determine a document's context if you have doubts about it.* There may be a good reason why a document appears anonymous. For instance, it may be a subdocument of a large publication at a Web site. Therefore, see if you can find the document's context. Often you need only look higher up the directory in the site's URL. For example, if you find a document with the URL

http://www.anyu.edu/faculty/research/ report2.html

remove **report2.html** from the URL and enter it into your browser. At that point you may see a menu, with links to documents, that describes what the document is about and who wrote it. Failing that, there may be other clues or links that will help you identify it.

- *Find corroborating documents.* Always look for other documents or sites about the same topic that provide supporting evidence to the point of view or facts presented in a document you want to use for your research. News reporters routinely look for corroborating evidence before running an investigative story. Even though there's no guarantee that if several people say the same thing, it's true, there's a better chance that it is. The search engines that have the option "find more documents like this one" will help you find corroborating information.

If you still have doubts about a document's validity, don't hesitate to show it to your teacher or professor. If she welcomes email from students, you may want to use the "mail document" function of your Web browser to send it directly to her.

Finally, make sure to cite the source of material from the Internet that you use in a project or research paper. Your school's or university's policies about academic honesty apply to electronic material as well as printed material. Unless you are told otherwise, use the same reference format you would use for print publications, and add the document's URL and the date you viewed it in parentheses at the end of the reference.

Key Concepts in This Chapter

- To locate information on the Internet you should develop strategies that draw on the various search engines we have explored, because one search engine will seldom be sufficient.

- You need to use different strategies to locate different kinds of information.

- To find factual information, first do a search with Altavista, then try other indexes; if necessary, revise your keywords and redo the searches; finally try searching newsgroups.

- To find Web sites, start by searching Yahoo!, browse some of its links, try other directories, and then as a last step search Altavista.

- To find reading material, begin with an Altavista search, move to other indexes, try specialized search tools such as library catalog indexes and Amazon.com, then search newsgroups.

- Always make sure to question the accuracy of material you find on the Web because there are no standards or safeguards for Web publishing.

LEARNING
THROUGH PROJECTS

CHAPTER 12

Projects on the Learning Highway

Some years ago, Volkswagen ran a television ad. It featured a man driving his VW to work in a snowstorm. The car stops, and the scene reveals the man getting out of his VW and getting into a snowplow. As the plow pulls away, a voice asks us to consider how the man who drives the snowplow drives *to* the snowplow.

At the Snowplow

In a way, "getting to the snowplow" is what you have done by reading this far—but now it is time to look at various learning projects that people have actually operated on the Internet. In some cases, we'll include descriptions of projects you can join; in others, we'll include the reflections that people have had about their own learning on the Internet.

Learning experiences on the Internet allow students to be taken seriously for what they have to say, and in this book's final section, we want to demonstrate how a sense of purpose and the desire to understand the experiences of others are really the keys to learning on the Internet. We also wish to show that having a clear sense of task and purpose provides a useful structure

and approach to Internet-based learning experiences.

Each project will be introduced in a way that links it to the various ideas we have explored in this book. We hope they convey those ideas in ways you can use as part of your Internet learning, either because there is a project here that you want to participate in, or because you will have a strong sense of *how to use* the Internet as a learning highway based on the examples provided here.

Numerous programs and learning networks are profiled, and each is introduced with some ideas about how it is, or could be, used for creating projects, incorporating Internet experiences into courses, or even how you might work with teachers who may not understand what the Internet is, or appreciate what value it might have to your school work.

At-a-Glance Profile

We also include a short profile at the beginning of each project description, which will look like this:

Title	Name of project
Level	Secondary, Post Secondary
Type	Focus on information; interaction; task; technology; research; class-to-class exchanges; etc.
Tool(s)	Email, listserv, Web, etc.
Contact	Email Address, Website

Looking at the Projects

There are many books about the Internet, and a good deal has been written about online education too. Many, if not most, of these publications are written for teachers, or post-secondary students and researchers who are actually studying online education. Your teachers may be interested in knowing more about online education. Linda Harasim, of Simon Fraser University in Canada, Judith B. Harris, of the University of Texas at Austin, and Robin Mason, of the Open University in the United Kingdom, have written extensively on the subject. The International Society for Technology in Education (ISTE), at the University of Oregon in the United States, also publishes educational journals and books in this area.

We mention these resources to you for two reasons. First, if you would like to help your teacher learn about ways to think of the Internet in education, then consider telling him or her about these resources (in addition to our book, of course!) Second, people like Linda Harasim and Judith Harris have identified a

number of categories to describe educational activities on the Internet.

Our categories are more general and we have tried to incorporate many of the experiences that others have identified by grouping them into four broad areas of focus. They are:

1. FOCUS ON INTERACTION

This includes using the Internet for activities that involve interaction or collaboration with others. For example:

- Penpals, or person-to-person exchanges

- Class-to-class exchanges

- "Ask-an-expert" or online guests

- Online field trips

- Problem-solving activities

- Understanding the computer as a catalyst for learning

2. FOCUS ON INFORMATION.

This includes using the Internet for activities like:

- Research (information searches, collection, and organization)

- Publishing or sharing research with others

3. FOCUS ON TASK

This includes using the Internet to focus on particular learning activities. For example:

- Writing

- Simulations

- Social Issues

4. FOCUS ON TECHNOLOGY

This includes Internet-based activities designed to promote:

- Learning about technology and its uses

- Understanding the computer as a tool

Project Descriptions

The following projects demonstrate the broad range of possibilities available on the Internet. The projects reflect a wide range of uses of communication and information retrieval technologies on the Internet—from electronic mail to computer-conferencing to the Web. But what is most important is that the Internet is capable of sustaining the many exciting ideas that you, as a student, have, and that you can participate in as an Internet learner.

We hope you enjoy them.

CHAPTER 13

Canadian World Fest and Blue Print Earth

by
Indu Varma
Marshview Middle School
Sackville, New Brunswick

Title	Canadian World Fest, Blue Print Earth
Level	Middle School, Secondary, Post-Secondary Teacher Education
Type	Focus on information; interaction; task
Tool(s)	Email, listserv, Web
Contact	Indu Varma, ivarma@nbnet.nb.ca http://cyberfair.gsn.org/ marshawk/index.html

Indu Varma writes:

The exciting thing about this and other online projects is that each year, with a new group of students, there are new and different activities on topics based on the interest of the students. Students learn through their explorations of the Internet, the sharing of information—first-hand—through direct communication with peers, and by examining each other's work.

Indu's students are well known in Canada's online community. Each year, they use the Internet to find information and to communicate with others. Communicating with students from this class at Marshview Middle School in Sackville, New Brunswick, reveals an important component of learning on the Internet—when it's done well, it's nothing out of the ordinary. It's just part of what you do.

Indu adds:

The people from the local community play a significant role as well, by teaching the students about important aspects of their culture. It is a unique way of learning. For example, we invited a Native person from Canada's Department of Indian Affairs to speak to us about Native culture. He gave the class a wealth of information. Coming from him it was authentic. The students were spellbound as they listened to him. I know that they will now be able to share their newfound knowledge about the culture of Micmac people in New Brunswick with others on the Internet.

These projects involve students at the middle-school level, but we wanted to include them here because the Marshview experience offers Internet students some useful insights into project design. Any student, at any level, who is seeking to establish an Internet project based on interaction and participation can benefit by reading tips from this group, and we would like to highlight a few of them here.

- The projects involve research and reporting, but when you look at the objectives for each of them, you will see that these are not the main reasons for involvement. The tasks are to consider issues associated with heritage, and the environment. Undertaking research and reporting to others provides the means by which these opportunities to learn are sustained.

- On the one hand, these projects offer flexibility in terms of the information that participants provide. On the other, they provide guidance and clear expectations in the form of specific tasks and timelines.

- Students in secondary school programs are likely to find projects like these especially useful because of the structure of classes at this level. The approach and design of these projects lend themselves well to regular contact with other students in your own classes because the online experience can become a component of classroom activity.

- Post-secondary students in teacher-education programs are also likely to find these projects useful for the same reasons, as they construct valuable learning experiences in their practice-teaching placements.

The project descriptions for Canadian World Fest and Blue Print Earth follow.

Many thanks to Indu Varma and the students of Marshview Middle School for telling us about their work.

Canadian World Fest: Be Proud of Who You Are—A Project on Heritage Between Schools Around the World

CANADA

Canada
A land of plenty,
Majestic,
Beautiful in its grandeur,
Built by many races, faces,
Nationalities, and cultures
From different pasts
Each seeking its place,
Striving for recognition,
Wishing a harmonious existence,
Working towards a golden future
Together.

OBJECTIVES
The main objective of this project is to generate an interest in heritage and culture among youth of the world by getting them involved in discovering, celebrating, and sharing their heritage and the various achievements of people in their respective communities.

SPECIFIC OBJECTIVES
1. Develop an awareness among students about

their rich cultural heritage, particularly their own past, their own customs, and the special achievements of their own community.

2. Generate an appreciation among our youth of other distinguished individuals and their special contributions toward the building of our nation.

3. Promote mutual understanding of our cultural differences, create racial harmony, develop bonds of friendship, and oneness among the present and future generations through this tele-linking of students from around the world.

4. Provide our youth with a unique opportunity to learn by teaching others about their cultural heritage and special traditions.

5. Create a feeling of pride by celebrating the Canadian achievements of various races, faces, and cultures who have built this country.

FORMAT

Schools around the world are invited to participate in this unique experience. The project runs for three weeks each year, generally during January and February. The schedule for this project, as well as other online projects, is posted on the Marshview Middle School's home page:

http://cyberfair.gsn.org/marshawk/index.html

The format for the *Canadian World Fest* project is as follows:

Week One: Creative Writing
The students prepare poems or stories describing their roots and their identity. The title of their creative writing includes the name of the

country of participating schools. For example, the stories and poems by the students at Marshview bear the title "I Am a Canadian," and mention Canadian places and activities.

Week Two: Famous People or Landmarks
The students create historical or biographical sketches of famous people or landmarks in their community, which bear the title "Did You Know?" They share with others their unique cultural heritage, the distinctive characteristics of their community, the special cultural traditions of the people in their area, and the important contributions made by these persons. The students often enclose pictures of well-known people and landmarks with their sketches so that these may be included on the Web page.

Week Three: Art and Culture
Students research the backgrounds of a group of people in their community, finding out about the group's art forms, dance, language, stories, food, or music, which form integral parts of their lives, and share this information with others. Pictures and descriptions often serve as an inspiration for original artwork. For example, the students at Marshview undertook research about Canada's Native people and learned how to create masks.

Blue Print Earth

OBJECTIVES
The main objective of *Blue Print Earth* is to provide an exciting educational opportunity that allows students to enhance their creative talents and use their imaginations to design gadgets, invent articles, and picture social or political scenarios that will make planet Earth a better place to live for future generations.

The project began in 1994, and runs during January and February each year. To check the exact time period, look at the schedule of online projects on Marshview Middle School's home page, or check the Blue Print Earth Web page located at:

http://www.kidlink.org:80/KIDFORUM/ Blue-97/#Time1

SPECIFIC OBJECTIVES:

1. Develop an awareness of the environmental and social problems that Earth's inhabitants face today; for example, destruction of the ozone layer, the effects of chemical sprays, the devastation of areas plagued by constant earthquakes and volcanic activity, child malnutrition.

2. Promote critical thinking and problem-solving abilities among our students by having them come up with solutions to the problems mentioned above.

3. Stimulate students' creativity and imaginations by involving them in designing and inventing gadgets or items to solve these problems.

4. Develop communication and interpersonal skills by marketing the designed products.

FORMAT

Schools across Canada and throughout the world may participate in *Blue Print Earth*. Each school is given a fictitious amount of $10,000 to spend on products designed by other schools that they believe will cure some of planet Earth's serious problems. The project runs for eight weeks, four of which are online. The format is as follows:

1. A dialogue among students about the most serious problems facing our planet will take place in the first week. Students from each school then post their list of serious problems, in order of their gravity, on the Internet.

2. During the second week a discussion about some of the possible solutions takes place between the participating schools. This is a brainstorming activity, intended to generate many possibilities.

3. Following the dialogue of the first two weeks, the students spend about three weeks developing products that they believe will provide possible solutions to the problems. During the sixth week of the project, the students go back online to describe their creations (e.g., a new type of helmet that absorbs UV rays, a brand of chewing gum that has fluoride in it, or a new type of interlocking brick used in construction to make buildings earthquake safe). They may post drawings or digitized pictures of their creations on the network.

4. During the seventh week, the students have the opportunity to buy and sell their creations, using their fictitious $10,000 to buy the gadgets they believe would provide the most useful, workable, and practical solutions. They also have the opportunity to market their own products using advertising, cartoons, brochures, and other strategies.

5. The set-up is similar to an auction, where bids are placed on objects—but the product is not "sold" to the highest bidder. Instead the product that accumulates the highest total of all the bids is declared the winner.

6. During the final week of the project, if possible, the students display their wares via a satellite broadcast linking up schools across the country and throughout the world. The winners (designers whose items gross the most money) will have a chance to exhibit their products and perhaps even explore the possibility of developing prototypes and having these manufactured.

CHAPTER 14

Canadian Home Page Olympics

by
Steve Skultety
Computer Resource Teacher
Cecil Rhodes School
Winnipeg, Ontario

Title	Canadian Home Page Olympics
Level	K–12
Type	Focus on information; technology
Tool(s)	Web
Contact	Steve Skultety skultety@MINET.gov.MB.CA

The Canadian Home Page Olympics *(CHPO) is a national competition in which students submit URLs of a Web site they have designed and posted on the Internet. These sites are judged, and the winners receive prizes donated by generous corporate sponsors who want to support the efforts of youth in learning about technology.*

CHPO seeks to promote entrepreneurship and technical skills, encouraging students to explore and utilize new perspectives and technology skills, and to see this as part of their learning, both in school and in the world of work. One of the aspects of CHPO that we liked was how the skills acquired in one context were applicable to another—something it shares with most of the projects profiled in The Learning Highway.

Steve Skultety, a computer resource teacher in Winnipeg, Manitoba, developed the proposal to operate CHPO and submitted it to Canada's SchoolNet, a national educational service, for funding and assistance. CHPO is hosted on the SchoolNet Web site (www.schoolnet.ca).

We would like to thank Steve for his work, both online and in this book.

As an educator, I feel that students will need a skill set relating to Internet technologies in the future. Given the phenomenal growth of the World Wide Web, and the increased role individuals who are familiar with its technologies will play in a more entrepreneurial economy, I wanted to challenge Canadian students to develop and hone their computer skills.

The key to a successful online project is developing sound educational goals. Far too often, educators allow technology to determine project goals rather than using it as a means to an end. As well, there must be sufficient technical skill on the part of the organizer, otherwise, no matter how worthwhile the goals, the project cannot be implemented. Finally, there must be easy and convenient access to online resources. When these three components are present, one has the beginnings of a successful Internet-based project. The Canadian Home Page Olympics, which began in 1996, was such a project.

HOW IT WORKS

The students have three weeks to design their Web sites. After this initial construction period, sites are accepted for judging over a four-week period. The contest opens in March and closes at the end of April.

I believe this competition should be a learning experience and that each student should have the same resources at his or her disposal. Each student is directed to a downloadable package containing an HTML primer, and the URLs of other software that will assist them in the construction of their Web pages. Links to Windows and Macintosh HTML editors and other Web-authoring programs are also provided, putting all novice students on a level playing-field.

The contest package includes the official entry form, a Web page which, when submitted, is passed to a PERL (Practical Extraction and Reporting Language) script. This action enters the student's name, school, and the site's URL to a database. The entry script is not activated until the contest begins in March, so early entries cannot be processed before this date. The results are posted at the end of May.

Students build their own Web sites. They may not be assisted by teachers or parents. However, teachers and parents are encouraged to assist students in gaining an understanding of how to use any programs that they may require to develop their entries, including HTML editors and utility programs. They can be taught how to use the programs, but not how to apply them to their own sites. Students are also responsible for acquiring space on a server to store their pages, though they may receive assistance with the uploading of their pages to the Internet.

REQUIRED ELEMENTS

Student entries in the CHPO must contain the following elements:

- The Web site must have a minimum of one original graphic.

- It must have at least one link that results in the movement to a different HTML document within the site. This document must also be of the student's own creation.

- The site must have a minimum of one link that will result in the movement to a different site not of the student's own design.

- Entries must be posted on the Internet and be accessible until the end of the school year.

Teachers without the necessary knowledge may be asked to take on a supportive role by students in this project. Consequently, an online resource was established during the 1996 CHPO. A site (including documentation) was posted outlining how to construct a basic home page. Links are also provided that point to other resources available on the Web.

REFLECTIONS

As the teacher, one of the most difficult aspects of the project for me was to develop the technical skills needed to implement the project. I had to learn many skills, the most difficult being CGI (Common Gateway Interface) programming in PERL, which allows an Internet server to run external programs. This was needed to handle the processing of the entries. When I submitted the proposal for CHPO to SchoolNet, I did not have the programming skills necessary to code the PERL scripts, but I was confident I could acquire them. And I did.

TRANSFERABLE SKILLS

Since then, the technical skills I have developed while running the CHPO have allowed me to develop or assist in developing other successful Internet projects. Educators must realize that the time they spend learning new technical skills will benefit them and their students. Unfortunately, there is never enough time for professional development, which means that some personal time may have to be sacrificed. This is an important consideration for teachers because they may find that this undertaking competes with the other demands teaching makes on time "outside" of school, like marking, extracurricular activities, field trips, and so on.

The many students who participated in the CHPO during its first two years benefited from the skills they learned from their teachers. I believe that educators should attempt to foster life-long learning in their students. Getting kids hooked on technology is a good way to achieve this. Because technology changes rapidly, learning must be continuous if one wants to keep up with the latest advances. Quite often, this takes the form of independent learning, another skill that I think students should possess, and that is transferrable to other endeavors. However, in the case of the Canadian Home Page Olympics, prizes were awarded in order to help motivate students to push the technical envelope, and to underscore that their work had value to educators, corporations, and other students.

Many students mentioned via email that the CHPO was an invaluable learning experience for them. By participating in this contest, they advanced their computer literacy skills. These skills, if developed sufficiently, can be used by students to market themselves. The winner of the Senior category in the CHPO '96, for example, was employed by his home municipality to develop a Web site, and he has since gone on to form his own computer-based business. Many students involved in the CHPO are actively involved in developing commercial Web sites.

The CHPO fostered the creation of student-developed, Canadian-based content for the Internet. The topics were diverse, educational, and entertaining. Web sites dealt with topics from astronomy to Java coding to women's hockey, and from oceans of the world to home improvement. Some of the sites were truly outstanding.

The CHPO has been a nine-month project over each of the last two years. In October the proposal was prepared and submitted to Canada's SchoolNet. Once the proposal was accepted, sponsors had to be solicited. This involved writing many more proposals, most of which were declined. This was quite disheartening as the contest started and we still didn't have the full complement of prizes to award. Finally,

Sun Microsystems, Apple Computers, Microsoft, and Canada's SchoolNet agreed to sponsor the project. Once the sponsors were found, permission to use company logos had to be obtained. At the same time, the contest Web site had to be developed, which outlined timelines, rules, and judging criteria. The downloadable entry package had to be designed for both Windows and Macintosh platforms. And coding the entry processing script also had to be done.

JUDGING

Once the contest opened, we took a short breather. But before it closed, judges had to be solicited, assigned a geographical region and an age category, and briefed on the judging criteria. Evaluation sheets had to be designed and distributed to the judges. When the contest closed, each judge assessed projects from the provinces they were assigned, submitting the URL of the top three sites in each. A master list was then compiled based on the results. This master list was in turn redistributed to all the judges. Using this list, judges picked their national top three Web sites in each category. Each judge submitted his or her top three national choices. Again a list was compiled. The judges then met to decide the winners by consensus. This process took a little over three

hours. Once the winners were determined, the contest Web site had to be updated. The names of the winners were posted with a link to their site. As well, there was a link to the database of all the sites entered.

After having read the judging criteria, one student built a whole new Web site, as he felt it would be better received by the judges than his first site due to its original content and choice of topic. Just before the entry deadline, he emailed me saying that it had almost killed him, but his site was finally done. His hard work paid off. His Web site was chosen as the best Junior Web site. It just so happened that with this distinction went a new SPARC workstation with a 17-inch monitor from Sun Microsystems.

The goal of the CHPO is to foster the development of skills relating to Web technologies among Canadian students in the hope that it will help participants compete in the workforce. From what I've seen during the judging process over the last two years, many Canadian students are well positioned for entering the economy of the future. I'm just glad I could participate in this contest without having to enter a Web site of my own.

CHAPTER 15

DOR-WEST: English as a Second Language/English as a Second Dialect

by
Carmelina Crupi and Natalie McNamara
Westview Centennial Secondary School
Toronto, Ontario

Title	DOR-WEST: ESL/ESD Conferencing Project
Level	Secondary, Post Secondary/Teacher Education
Type	Focus on interaction; task
Tool(s)	Email, computer-conferencing
Contact	Carmelina Crupi and Natalie McNamara Carm@edu.yorku.ca

The DOR-WEST project will interest student teachers (and, no doubt, students who are taught by student teachers) who wish to develop online learning initiatives to meet particular student needs. In this chapter, Carmelina Crupi and Natalie McNamara describe how they developed their project in order to address the needs of a group of ESL and ESD students at their sponsor school.

Neither Carmelina nor Natalie had used computer technology in their teaching before. They were drawn to the Internet because of the needs they wanted to address in their sponsor school, not because they wished to promote Internet use.

Like some of the other projects described in The Learning Highway, *such as* Dramapolooza *and the* Canadian Home Page Olympics, *DOR-WEST provides a good example of how a first project can develop. A simple idea and a worthy task are powerful ingredients when it comes to learning online.*

One of the ways this is revealed is in how Carm and Natalie were "surprised" by the things they learned from their students in the online conferences. However, they were not so surprised that they lost sight of their original aims and aspirations. Rather, they came to understand them—and their own teaching—in new ways. As they point out:

> *It is true that similar objectives can be met without the computer. After all, the pedagogical principles underlying the DOR-WEST project are not unique to the technological*

classroom but have, in fact, been used in second-language classrooms for years. The advantage of such a project is that many of these traditional classroom principles— among them, co-operative learning, group work, and independent study—are integrated in computer conferencing.

In 1996, the DOR-WEST project received an honorable mention from the International Society for Technology in Education, University of Oregon, in their annual Telecomputing Activity Plan *contest.*

Many thanks to Carmelina and Natalie for describing it here.

DOR-WEST was a teleconferencing project undertaken in the 1994–95 school year to encourage language proficiency among English as a Second Language (ESL) and English as a Second Dialect (ESD) students. The project linked students at our practicum site, Westview Centennial Secondary School in the Jane-Finch area—a major Metro Toronto reception area for recent migrants, immigrants, and refugees— with a similar group at École secondaire Dorval in Montreal. Over 70 percent of our students at Westview were not Canadian-born, and the student population represented more than sixty countries and language groups. Both Dorval and Westview students shared the challenge of adapting to a new country and surviving in a large urban environment.

In ESL/ESD instruction, the classes are divided on the basis of fluency rather than age. Westview's ESD level-four students were recent Caribbean immigrants who experienced some Creole interference in oral and written standard English. Dorval's ESL secondary level-five stu-

dents spoke English fluently and may have studied English before immigrating to Quebec.

In summary, the project involved a series of teleconferences between students at Westview and Dorval. Each conference dealt with a different theme such as identity, change, choices, relationships, and conflict. It is important to recognize, however, that a project such as DOR-WEST can be modified to suit any classroom whatever the ability levels of the students.

Since time was of utmost concern to both the students and teachers involved, we decided to limit the project to three or four hours per week. (This was not difficult because we chose thematic units that were already part of the course curriculum.) One seventy-five-minute period was used for final editing and posting the students' written work online. Independent lab times were also scheduled (approximately two hours per week) for the posting of those messages beyond the minimum requirements of the project.

The DOR-WEST project was the perfect initiation for the technophobes involved (student teachers and students alike!). The hardware and software requirements were minimal, and the project was easily adapted to the available resources in our school. We used ClarisWorks on a Macintosh Classic II. For teleconferencing purposes, we used FirstClass Communications Software and a 2400 baud modem. Any word processing and teleconferencing software will serve similar projects equally well.

Due to language barriers, ESL/ESD students experience an absence of voice that discourages writing. As student teachers, we shared the belief that the students would explore an unfamiliar territory (writing in standard English) if they were allowed to discuss familiar territory (their own cultural backgrounds). The DOR-WEST project was based on an interactive approach that values collaboration and meaningful communication as tools for learning. It was designed to match ESL/ESD students from two diverse student populations in order to expand their knowledge of various cultures and increase their overall fluency in English. In addition, the program was created to raise students' reading and writing proficiencies and to encourage them to develop critical-thinking skills.

The procedure and assignment requirements were simple. To begin with, each student was asked to submit a brief welcome message, which served to introduce him or her to the rest of the conference participants. Then they had to write at least two formal compositions to be posted online; the compositions focused on the following topics: Countries of Origin (a conference that encouraged an awareness of identity, multiculturalism, and tolerance); Discrimination (a forum to discuss personal experiences, opinions, and concerns); Future Goals (a conference where students were to articulate choices, dreams, and aims for the future); My Neighborhood (an arena to discuss community, relationships, and concerns); Storytelling (encouraged exchange of both oral and literary traditions); and Recreation (a forum for sports, music, and other personal interests). In addition to these requirements, students were encouraged to develop an ongoing correspondence with their peers at the partner school.

The mixture of both formal and more conver-sational writing was quite deliberate. Language is better acquired when students engage in practical and meaningful tasks that require a synthesis of language strategies. Thematic units provide the context for such activities. With this model, the learning becomes more student-directed and the teacher's role becomes one of facilitator and monitor.

With this project, then, the role of the teacher was that of moderator. As moderators, we organized the conference. However, it was the feedback that kept the students online. The online feedback given was not unlike that offered by teachers and students with the use of classroom response journals. Feedback included suggestions for elaboration, questions to encourage debate, as well as summaries and clarification of threads of discussion that arose from time to time.

To generate discussion and encourage participation, we initially posted questions in each of the topic folders. For example, the folder entitled "Oral Storytelling" included the following questions under the initial posting "Welcome to Storytelling": "Did someone ever tell you a story you enjoyed so much that you wanted to tell it to someone else? Why was it special? Did it talk about something that you value?" With these prompts, we were trying to encourage cultural appreciation for the oral traditions of the students while presenting a basis for the comparison of written standard English and spoken Caribbean dialects. The final question forced the students to think critically about the importance of their chosen story.

The folder entitled "Discrimination" began with the following moderator's message:

"People may experience discrimination because of gender (whether someone is male or female), culture, or religion. If you choose to write about the topic of 'Discrimination,' think about these questions: Have you or anyone close to you experienced some kind of discrimination? How did the experience make you feel? How did you react to the situation? Is there anything you could do to change or prevent the experience from happening again?" There are two things worth mentioning here. As student teachers, we expected to see numerous postings related to cultural discrimination. To our surprise, there were an equal number of postings related to age discrimination—a category we neglected to include in our original list. We quickly responded to the authors of those postings and thanked them for bringing age into the discussion. Second, we decided to use more sophisticated terms such as "gender" (as opposed to "sex") with a definition provided in parenthesis because we felt that students needed exposure to more sophisticated vocabulary.

Eliminating linguistic barriers and providing opportunities for independent work go hand in hand. Technical computer jargon is confusing enough for native English speakers; it is that much more complicated for the second-language learner. We found graphical illustrations of the computer screen accompanied by simple step-by-step instructions extremely helpful. By simply selecting the "Print Screen" button on the computer, we received instructional materials. Students were able to see exactly what they would be viewing on the computer screen. On days when we did not have access to the computer lab, this was an invaluable way to have a "computer lesson" without the comput-

ers. In addition, students were able to refer independently to the instructional sheets whenever they needed a reminder about how to send email, change fonts, or simply log in.

This project provided "virtual independence." The main difference between response journals and this type of project was that all feedback was available to all participants. Because of this, it was necessary that teachers moderate in "moderation." Some moderating needed to be done by the students themselves; if students were not understood by their fellow students, clarification was asked for, and received. The students needed to know that they could be understood by their peers and not just their own teachers. Ultimately, the students must leave our classrooms and be able to use their language skills independently.

Instructors who are weary of "educational bandwagons" may wonder whether it is worth the effort of incorporating technology in teaching. It is true that similar objectives can be met without the computer. After all, the pedagogical principles underlying the DOR-WEST project are not unique to the technological classroom but have, in fact, been used in second-language classrooms for years. The advantage of such a project is that many of these traditional principles—among them, cooperative learning, group work, and independent study—are integrated in computer-conferencing. We have seen time and time again that students become lifelong learners when they are given the opportunity to assume responsibility for their own learning. This is only possible when the teacher becomes a facilitator (in this case as an online monitor) who shows the students how to learn rather than what to learn. In a time when teachers are constantly called on to move toward an integrated rather than a specialist curriculum, projects such as DOR-WEST, which successfully integrate literacy, computer skills, and cultural studies, are an effective way to meet educational outcomes despite time constraints. Online evaluation of learning can be conducted daily, which allows for consistent feedback to the student. The "published and polished" look of computer-generated writing gives students a sense that their work has dignity and value.

Finally, and perhaps most important, a project such as DOR-WEST allows students with differing degrees of language proficiency to interact successfully and learn from one another.

CHAPTER 16

Dramapolooza: Scenes across the Net—Hands across the Water

by
Laurence Siegel
David and Mary Thompson Collegiate Institute
Scarborough, Ontario

Title	Dramapolooza: Scenes across the Net—Hands across the Water
Level	Secondary
Type	Focus on interaction; task
Tool(s)	Email, listserv
Contact	Laurence Siegel Laurence_Siegel@sbe.scarborough.on.ca

Laurence Siegel called Trevor Owen one day with an idea. His senior drama class had been working on some original scenes with a visiting playwright, and he had been thinking about putting their work online. He wanted to know what approaches might be feasible and whether Owen would help his class develop a project. Owen thought it was a terrific idea and was eager to get involved.

As the project unfolded over the term, he thought their experiences would be useful to readers of The Learning Highway *for two reasons:*

- *First, neither Siegel nor the students had ever participated in an Internet project before, so its development could be followed from beginning to end.*

- *Second, when the project finished, issues of success or failure were not as clear cut as one might have expected. Did this project actually "work"? What constitutes success in online learning initiatives?*

The Dramapolooza *project presents the kind of useful—and real—questions that most new projects face. They are questions that go beyond technical concerns like "How do I connect?" or "Where do I post my project online?" They involve more pressing concerns, like "What things matter when Internet learning actually arrives in the classroom?"*

Owen writes:

> *When I invited Laurence to contribute to this book, I had not considered what impact my own participation in the project might*

have—on the students' learning or on my own. But when some of the students reported their views on my involvement in their project, I saw quite clearly how some of the ideas in this book also apply to me. The main one is the value and power of listening. Many of the ideas we seek to promote in The Learning Highway—*the value of purpose, relationship, and interaction in Internet learning—are really forms of "listening" or taking seriously the ideas of those with whom one works. This skill is transferable, and applies as much to face-to-face interaction in the classroom as it does online.*

Many thanks to Laurence and the drama class at David and Mary Thompson C.I. in Scarborough, Ontario, for reminding us of this.

Over the past thirty years, the discipline of dramatic arts has evolved and changed direction. Introduced in the curriculum as "theater arts," drama programs tended to emphasize performance and production-based skills. In many cases our interest in doing theater was so intense and the kids' response so rewarding that we were able to overlook some of the richness of our work—the process and the potential for dramatic arts to become a focus for exploring content and issues across the curriculum. But the dynamics of content and process slowly evolved into a broader and more inclusive vision of drama in education. Instead of simply emphasizing aesthetic excellence, drama became a base for exploring issues and values in the lives of teenagers. One of the strengths of dramatic arts in the curriculum is its ability to help students develop skills and explore values through role playing and imagination. And drama can be used to interpret other disci-

plines. Its flexibility and adaptability make it an attractive and useful classroom tool.

DRAMA AND TECHNOLOGY

How can we, in an age of burgeoning technology, use the Internet and the World Wide Web to bring drama into play. The challenge is to bring the personal, reflective, and aesthetic aspects of drama and the technical skills and applications of computers together. Our project provided such an opportunity.

The opportunity to use the Internet is almost irresistible. It's a new toy to many of the students and their teachers. And so we approach the new toy with itchy fingers. In our excitement, we have to be careful about the marriage between content and process. The latter can get lost in the former because the bells and whistles of technology are so enticing.

ENTER DRAMAPOLOOZA

Here's how our project happened: We began, as we had a year earlier, by bringing in a Governor General's Award-winning playwright, Jason Sherman. This was to be our Canadian unit.

Jason opened the writing workshop by asking students, "What irks you?" They thought about it and here's what they came up with: unreasonable rules, loss, death, the confusing demands of relationships, sex, pregnancy, parents—and their absence, unrealized dreams, trust and mistrust.

Jason helped the students to incorporate these themes into dramatic scenes through writing, reading, critique, rewriting, and talk—lots of talk. What were the scenes about? What were the important words and ideas? What did we think was unimportant? That was hard. The students did not want to edit their own work at first. But they were brutal with the work of their peers. They saw flaws in the scenes other students wrote.

Jason worked with the students every other day for two weeks. Our time with him was limited because we had only enough money to hire him for a few sessions. We found that when his time with us was over, we had not completed our task. We did not have a play. But Jason had helped us put the scenes together as a performance. It was rough, but it was a start, and we worked on it on our own for a few more days until we were ready to present it.

It was the performance that made the students think there might be more in this project than the writing and a one-shot performance. During the first few days following Jason's departure, the work proceeded quickly. And by the third day, the depth of the work began to emerge. The students began to tell stories of betrayal, doubt, loss, and fear. One girl spoke of being demeaned by friends and family because she dreamed of making action movies. Another girl talked about a troubled long-distance relationship and one young man spoke of the anguish of his father's death, which was intensified by a mother who seemed to nag at him out of her need to deny. Yet another talked about, and then wrote a scene about, a friend who revealed his homosexuality during a hockey tournament.

The maturity and seriousness of the discussions raised the students' respect for one another. We had the basis for a play—a set of scenes based on personal themes that would form an anthology. The students decided the scenes would be

played as examples of screenplay ideas pitched by an aspiring and not-to-be-put-off screenwriter to a hard-edged seen-it-all producer.

Was our play successful? Yes, relatively. Yet there was an air of disappointment and letdown in the performance. It wasn't as exciting as it appeared on paper or in discussion and critique. We talked about this, and the students identified a gap between the imagined creation and the actual production.

They became aware of the richness of their imagination and the limitations imposed by our circumstances—the small performance space, the lack of technical facilities, the shortage of time, the constraints imposed by the variety of relationships among our group of fifteen people, the varying degrees of commitment and talent. But the biggest limitation was having to produce a play within a two-week period.

How could these scenes take on a life that would satisfy and warm the hearts of their creators? The answer proved elusive. The students knew they needed to see the play as interpreted by others. The solution was the Net.

We got there with some trepidation. One student called Ryan said: "I can understand why some [of the students] would feel exposed by releasing their scenes into a cyber-world full of criticism.... A person's writing is deeply personal, it takes courage to allow strangers, let alone friends, to edit it as they see fit."

ANOTHER EXPERT ARRIVES
Deciding to go to the Net gave us the opportunity to bring in one of the authors of this book, Trevor Owen. I wanted to have the students work with yet another expert. I wanted them to

sense the value of their work through the participation of people outside the school in the professional community. Enter Trevor. His arrival and interaction with the class spurred them on, giving them new energy as they envisioned the play being read by interested and like-minded strangers. A student called Sabrina said:

> We produced some excellent and extraordinary pieces that all of us could be proud of. We met Trevor Owen, who would be assisting us in putting our work on the Internet for others to read. Mr. Owen's attitude...he listened to us, made us feel comfortable, and he treated us as equals. That's something you can respect, no matter who you are. When it was time to put our work on the Internet, I was excited and thrilled.... I also had some anxiety about the responses I might get. However, my excitement and anticipation overpowered my doubts.

When the students had their scenes written, critiqued, and ready to send off, they wrote a "teaser" to advertise the work:

> What do you get when you put 15 senior drama students together with a nationally celebrated writer, writing a series of personally based scenes about relationships, teenagers, sex, parents, death, AIDS, dating...? You get Dramapolooza. Want to see the work? Get in touch, we'd love to show it to you.

We emailed our notice to a listserv on Canada's SchoolNet. It didn't take long. Two schools replied within a few days.

My students had two reactions. First, they had not really expected any replies. I have wondered whether this may have to do with their inexperience at writing, or whether they did not actually value their own work. In part, their unfamiliarity with plays and playwriting may be a factor here. They are unaware of the impact of conversation and conflict as the subject of short prose. They are likely more familiar with novels and formal essays as written forms.

The students' second reaction was amazement. This was not only because we *received* a response, but because the responses had come from afar, from Guam and Australia.

As teachers, we are bombarded with the idea that our students are worldly and aware. But many, I find, are quite sheltered. They may feel pressured to be worldly. They may be frightened about appearing provincial. The world may be moving so fast that it is all they can do to pretend to be keeping up. So much to know, so little time, with school, friends, part-time jobs, stress at home....

But clearly, they did not know about Guam, where it was, what kind of people lived there, what the weather was like, or what its significance was in World War II. The project gave them the opportunity not only to learn about Guam but also to learn about their own apparent isolation.

> When we put our work on the Internet, I was interested in seeing what people across the world would think about the work I was so proud of. Unfortunately we never did get a response, which was disappointing, but I was happy to share my life experience with the others in my class and on the Internet.

[In fact, we did get responses, but the school in Guam that picked up our work did not ever get back to us after we sent it on.] (Heather)

The Internet, plays, books, reading, writing, television, and talk are all part of the communication arsenal of today's teenagers. They use some of these things well. Certainly, they have access to more forms of media than past generations, and they have it all at their fingertips. The choice is formidable, possibly overwhelming, and certainly stimulating. Their work is filled with cross-references from music, movies, news. Their lives are electronic.

While it may seem incongruous, it is also intriguing that their sense of self-esteem and identity can be enhanced by working with the Net. It is not an intimate instrument, like a book, which can be held while read with a parent or friend, or while one sits alone in a chair. But it can offer, as it did in our project, the excitement of travel, the opportunity to make a new friend, and the risk of uncertainty that what has been sent "out there" will be received by others with as much interest as we would like it to be. As one student concluded, "All in all, these were some very good life lessons. There are many different kinds of people in the world....We may not be happy with what we encounter, but we always come away as better people if we try to learn something from our experiences."

CHAPTER 17

Nadine Gordimer Internet Project

by R.W. Burniske
University of Texas at Austin
Austin, Texas

Title	Nadine Gordimer Internet Project
Level	Secondary
Type	Focus on information; task
Tool(s)	Email, listserv
Contact	R.W. Burniske burniske@mail.utexas.edu http://www.cwrl.utexas.edu/~burniske/eped

"Imagine students reading a short story set in South Africa, then corresponding with people in that country to discuss questions the story prompts," writes Richard (Buddy) Burniske. *"Less than a decade ago, political sanctions and exorbitant telephone fees would have frustrated such an endeavor. Now, however, this scenario is both imaginable and affordable for educators who are acquainted with telecomputing, and patient enough to meet its challenges."*

As Buddy reminds us in this piece, though, some of these challenges have as much to do with planning and setting realistic expectations as they do with technology.

There are many good things about this project. For example, it grew out of another project that Buddy described in the last edition of The Learning Highway. *This is important because it underscores how Internet learning can create new opportunities.*

In 1996, this project received an honorable mention in the annual Telecomputing Activity Plan Contest, *operated by the International Society for Technology in Education (ISTE) at the University of Oregon (Eugene). It focuses on using the Internet to study the works of the acclaimed South African author and Nobel laureate Nadine Gordimer. We think it will interest students of literature at both the secondary and post-secondary levels, as well as student teachers, who may be seeking useful online structures with which to approach literature.*

Many thanks to Buddy for telling us about the Nadine Gordimer Internet Project *here.*

I. BACKGROUND

At the time the first edition of *The Learning*

Highway was published, when I was a teacher at the International School of Kuala Lumpur, I described the South African Elections '94 Internet Project, a telecomputing activity that Lowell Monke, of the Des Moines Public Schools in the United States, and I created for high-school students to correspond with eye-witnesses during those historic elections. That project, which also attracted participants from North America, Europe, and South Africa, enabled students to participate in an historic moment vicariously. Inspired by that experience, and hoping the interest it had aroused would support a related undertaking, I initiated the Nadine Gordimer Short Story Project at the start of the following school year. I wanted students in various parts of the world to read the same stories by the 1991 Nobel laureate, then exchange interpretations of the stories and work toward a deeper understanding of them, as well as their respective viewpoints. Timing was problematic, however, and access to a common text impossible; we heard from students in Japan briefly, and enjoyed a fitful correspondence with South Africans, but never gathered the momentum necessary for dialogues to flourish.

A year later, however, after visiting South Africa to meet some of the people with whom I had become a "virtual colleague," I was determined to re-invent the proverbial wheel. I had learned a great deal about South African schools, from curricular constraints to academic calendars, and felt more confident about arranging a mutually beneficial project. I was also less naive about the notion of a "global village" than I had previously been. The success of a global telecomputing project, I had

learned, had as much to do with proper planning and establishing realistic expectations as it did with computer hardware and software. We would have to work collaboratively to accommodate our respective schedules, curricula, and students. Thus, I broadcast a call for participation on the South African schools network a few weeks before our school year was to begin. Interested teachers responded from a black township in Port Alfred, a "colored" school in Durban, and white private schools in Queenstown, Pretoria, and Grahamstown. Clearly, South Africans were interested in the project. But what would we do differently this time to improve our chances for success?

II. THE AIM

As a language-arts teacher I wanted to bring stories from another place and culture to life. I had previously employed videotapes and a variety of library resources to supplement the study of world literature. This time, however, I wanted to experiment with telecommunications, invigorating discussion of stories from South Africa through correspondence with students who lived there. I was teaching Introduction to Literary Analysis, an advanced English course for high-school sophomores. I wanted to introduce them to electronic mail and listserv communication to plant the seeds for a more sophisticated project I hoped to undertake later in the year. Along the way I wanted to invent better strategies for using telecommunications to enrich the study of fiction while challenging my students' skills as readers, writers, and thinkers.

We began with historical research of South Africa and discussion of Nadine Gordimer's fiction, refining skills as critical readers and writers. In addition to examining the conventions of the short story, we discussed the relevance of these stories in a post-apartheid South Africa. I asked students if these were timeless, universal stories or historical documents relying more upon a specific time and place than universal theme. What's more, how might present circumstances, the most current events, affect one's experience of stories written in previous decades? These were questions that I could not answer; one needed a much deeper understanding of South Africa's people and history, the kind that comes only through prolonged engagement or residence. What I wished to emphasize, and what I hoped my students would come to appreciate, was the significance of telecommunications as a tool for animating literature and addressing difficult questions. The following quotation served as a starting point:

> What I am saying is that I see that many of these stories could not have been written later or earlier than they were. If I could have juggled them around in the contents list of this collection without that being evident, they would have been false in some way important to me as a writer. What I am also saying, then, is that in a certain sense a writer is "selected" by his subject—his subject being the consciousness of his own era.

—Nadine Gordimer, Introduction to
Selected Stories

III. THE STRUCTURE

To provide structure, as well as limit the chaos of email correspondence, I created Story Element groups, with students specializing in one of the following categories:

1. Point of View/Character—Example: Why do you think Gordimer chose this point of view/protagonist for her story? Is this view/character universal or somehow unique to South Africa at that time? Are the characters one-dimensional or well developed? Why?

2. Setting—Example: How is setting crucial to the story? Research both the time and place in which the story is set. What significant events occurred during this decade?

3. Conflict/Resolution—Example: How does the conflict arise? Is it an internal or external conflict? Which elements contribute to it most significantly? Is the resolution of the conflict satisfying? Why or why not?

4. Writing Style and Structure (Plot)—How would you describe the style of this story: Diction? Sentence structure? Figurative language? Imagery? Tone? Quote passages. Is this style appropriate? Strengths/weaknesses? What about the story's design as a whole?

5. Theme—Example: What is the point of the story and what leads you to this conclusion? Is it possible to reduce the story to a single point? If so, is it universal? Quote passages that are especially significant to theme.

IV. REPORTS

Each group was responsible for drafting one weekly report. These documents, a pastiche of individual group members' writings, were limited to 350 words to encourage careful revision and concise prose. Reports consisted of three primary components:

1. *Analysis.* Brief analysis of the respective

story element was the starting point. We could not be certain the South African students would be familiar with the stories, however, so students needed to contextualize their remarks, balancing plot synopsis with critical analysis. The tension arising from this encouraged students to become discriminating readers and writers, debating which information was essential.

2. *Why Questions.* Students offered three Why questions that the story prompted, stimulating discussion rather than stifling it with What questions, which led to summary and premature closure. This proved essential to our dialogues. Without good questions the discussions were doomed. Unfortunately, most students were accustomed to teachers asking the questions, but with time they learned how to do this.

3. *Dear South Africa.* Finally, students prepared a brief letter to South Africans, asking about concerns a particular story raised. Example: "Is miscegenation illegal in post-apartheid RSA?" This encouraged students to think critically, asking questions that were pertinent to the story yet required the insight of a South African resident. We devoted class time to the creation, revision, and discussion of good questions, and returned to this issue periodically. Ultimately, correspondence via the limited bandwidth of electronic mail compelled students to write thoughtfully, revise carefully, and think continually.

V. SELECTED STORIES
I selected stories from three different decades, working chronologically toward the present, and the time period that our South African cor-

respondents would address. Each of my students was expected to read every story, but the labor of writing reports was divided among three classes. Thus, the respective classes were responsible for submitting three full reports to a project listserv, then corresponding with South Africans who chose to reply to their letter. This encouraged in-depth study of particular stories as well as a breadth of knowledge about Nadine Gordimer's work. Students in South Africa, meanwhile, would not be required to read Gordimer's stories, since many of them lacked an anthology of her work, but would serve as "experts" on current events and conditions in post-apartheid South Africa. In this way, we avoided the problems experienced in the pilot project, creating a mutually beneficial relationship without placing undue burdens upon students and teachers adhering to a prescribed curriculum. The reading schedule for my students was as follows:

Week 1—(1950s)
—"Six Feet of the Country" (Class #1)
—"Which New Era Would That Be?" (Class #2)
—"The Last Kiss" (Class #3)

Week 2—(1960s)
—"A Chip of Glass Ruby" (Class #1)
—"Some Monday for Sure" (Class #2)
—"The African Magician" (Class #3)

Week 3—(1970s)
—"Open House" (Class #1)
—"The Life of the Imagination" (Class #2)
—"Africa Emergent" (Class #3)

VI. ASSESSMENT
Student work was assessed on both an individual and group basis: Reading Journal (25%),

Class discussion/work (25%), Reports/Email (50%). Prior to our first class of the week, students were required to write an analysis of their assigned element and a list of Why questions that they wanted others to address. This exercise was completed in their Reading Journals, which served as a record of their thinking and analysis prior to group discussion. Their efforts to collaborate with group members and revise the pastiche that grew out of their individual writings constituted the other portion of their individual assessment. The entire group received holistic grades for their reports and credit for email exchanges. I did not scrutinize the latter, however, out of respect for correspondence and fear that it would discourage students from taking risks or engaging in natural discourse.

VII. REFLECTIONS

The Nadine Gordimer Internet Project presented unique challenges for us all. Not only did it require good, critical reading of the short stories, but also thoughtful, analytical writing. The dialogues with South African students enriched our classroom discussions, vivifying Gordimer's work while placing positive demands upon my students. Failing to complete an assignment meant disappointing classmates, who depended upon contributions to a group report, which in turn squandered opportunities to ask South African correspondents important questions. The delay between submission of reports and the replies from South Africans, some of whom had only one computer terminal linked to the

Internet and submitted reports through a single, shared email account, required patience from my students. What's more, it demanded that they not simply file a report and move on to the next story, forgetting previous stories or analyses. In this manner, the project offered a more authentic learning experience, with students coaxing one another to be more specific or critical, revisiting earlier work to clarify their observations or questions, rather than awaiting the teacher's instructions.

This is not to say that the classroom teacher's transition from "sage on the stage" to "guide on the side" is an easy one. I expended considerable time and energy designing the project and recruiting South African participants, then found myself coordinating an enterprise that involved half a dozen faculty members in as many locations, with mixed age groups and disciplines. Meanwhile, I also had to fulfill a prescribed course curriculum, one requiring a brisk pace through literary genres. Time was a relentless tyrant, and had I to do it again, I would allow two weeks for each report, thus providing more time for exchanges, though it would mean violating the curriculum I inherited. Ultimately, global telecomputing activities must be designed to accommodate a wide range of students, abilities, technical competence, technological affordances, schedules, and curricula. Attempting to create a "global village" is a commendable goal, but it is not a simple matter.

CHAPTER 18

The Gudmundstad School Project

by
Terje Kristensen
Associate Professor
Department of Computer Science
Bergen College
Landås, Norway

Title	The *Gudmundstad* School Project
Level	Secondary, Post Secondary
Type	Focus on information; technology
Tool(s)	Email, listserv, Web
Contact	Terje Kristensen terje@lsv.hib.no http://www.lsv.hib.no/ans/terje

We have seen how access to the Internet is often a major obstacle for schools. In North America, more and more schools are able to arrange their own access through commercial networks, as well as through networks established by education councils and authorities.

In other cases, though, links to the Internet are established in co-operation with post-secondary institutions. This arrangement can place post-secondary institutions in a difficult position because they are often not equipped with the resources necessary to support programs at schools in their regions. But there are also many examples of relationships that have been established between secondary and post-secondary institutions that serve the interests of both.

A number of projects featured in this book are supported by networks (e.g., I*EARN, Canada's SchoolNet), and we thought it would be useful to look at one in The Learning Highway.

This one, from Norway, comes to us from Terje Kristensen, who teaches at Bergen College. This project provides useful insights into the development and growth of a learning network, from fairly specific, local initiatives to regional, national, and even international ones.

Our thanks to Terje for describing the Gudmundstad learning environment in Norway.

BACKGROUND

Early in 1991 schools from different geographical parts of Bergen, Norway, were connected by modem to the server at our college. Each school was given a password and a username. When the pupils logged into our system, they had access to the email service there. In the beginning only eight schools participated, but this number has grown. Now the schools are connected by a special modem server, which lets the schools communicate more easily.

The students who participated in this early phase of our project came from fifth class and upward. The goal of our project was to let as many teachers as possible participate, even if they did not know much about computers and computer science. We also wanted the project to be integrated into different subjects at the schools.

The network of schools was used to gather meteorological data at different places in and near Bergen. The students were doing the observations themselves and each school sent the data they collected to all the others. Variables like wind direction, wind strength, rainfall, temperature, and type of weather were measured. To manipulate the meteorological measurements we developed a database program in *Prolog*, which allowed students and teachers to get an overview of the weather conditions in their location. They could also see the differences in local weather conditions around Bergen.

This phase of our project continued from 1991 until the end of 1994. The schools in the Bergen region established their links to the Internet in this way. At the time, this was quite a new experience for the schools in our region and in many ways it was a pioneering project. Having

access to the Internet through our college meant schools were able to make many national and international contacts to exchange ideas and knowledge. Many of the teachers who participated in the project at that time had never used a computer before, but both they and the students learned very quickly, and they were surprised how easy it was to send and receive messages by email.

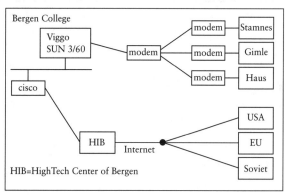

The pedagogical network of schools in the region of Bergen from 1991–94.

IMPACT ON LEARNING

The teachers and pupils who participated in the project were all very enthusiastic about this type of learning. The pupils were doing weather observations themselves, and running the database program to manipulate the data of the weather observations at different places around Bergen. They were eager to do the work and were discussing problems all the time with pupils at the other schools via email. Some of the schools imported the observations into spreadsheets and represented the data graphically.

At one school they arranged an "integrated day" in connection with the project. A whole day was taken to integrate the project into several subjects, like mathematics, science, and social studies, so the subject of meteorology was seen from many perspectives. In mathematics the weather observations were used to illustrate how spreadsheets work and how the data could be used to illustrate diagrams and statistics. The weather forecasting office in Bergen was also contacted and the pupils were given an orientation about how modern weather observations are done by advanced computers.

At another school the project was nicely integrated into geography. When they had information about the Baltic states, they contacted students from these countries. In this way they made the geography lesson become alive. The students discussed local problems and learned that they had much in common.

The project was also used in English education. Excellent contacts were established between an English class at Vaksdal, a local community, and a class in a school in Cleveland, Ohio. The students had regular contact with each other and discussed topics like the Gulf War and changes that were taking place in the former Soviet Union. Our experience is that foreign contacts gave language education a new dimension as the students learned many new words and sentences through their participation in the project. Later on, the students used IRC (Internet Relay Chat) to "talk" to each other.

One teacher who participated in the project talked about the Prolog program in mathematics and used it to give a short introduction to logic. The historical development of Prolog goes back to Aristotle, circa 330 B.C., when he developed his syllogism theory. An example of a syllogism is:

All men are mortal.

Socrates is a man.

Then Socrates is mortal.

Some teachers also talked about how logic could be used to both program computers and build databases. The students could then see how a database works in a computer program. Small examples of computer programs in Prolog were also demonstrated.

A NEW PHASE

The first phase of our project lasted until the end of 1994, and involved many schools from our region of Norway. Both students and teachers learned that email was an effective communication tool. Many contacts between schools in Bergen, Europe, and elsewhere around the world were developed in these years. The students used this new medium to gather different types of information, and teachers and students learned firsthand that they could work on different local and global school projects, even if they were separated geographically.

World Wide Web

In January 1995, a new phase in our project started. The initiative for this project phase was taken by Bjørn Lyngedal at Hav high school in Hordaland, Paal Thuland at Bergen College, and myself. The project continued as a cooperative venture between Bergen College, schools in Hordaland county, and Skrivervik Data, the vendor of Sun Microsystems in Norway, which sponsored our project with a SPARC station of ten UNIX machines. Two students in the engineering department of computer science at our college configured this machine as a WWW-server for the schools of our region as their final main project.

Our project is based on a certain view of technological infrastructure. The most important principle in this view is *openness* and the best exponent of this view has been expressed by our corporate partner, Sun Microsystems. Their philosophy of computing is that "the network is the computer" and, now that we have incorporated the use of the World Wide Web, we have come to understand how to implement this thinking by using the new programming language Java. From my point of view the stand-alone computer is not so important, but as part of a global network it gives us great possibilities to use in education.

A Centralized Technological Model

We have built an educational system for our region based on the principle of openness. Established industrial standards constitute the basis of this concept. This includes Ethernet computer networking, UNIX operating system (a popular operating system for multiple-user computers which has been important in the development of the Internet), TCP/IP (the collection of standards for communication between computers on the Internet), and the World Wide Web. In this model, local area networks (LAN) at different schools are connected to the Internet by an ISDN (Integrated Services Digital Network, sends digital signals over phone lines), a communication technology that is currently being introduced all over the country by Norwegian Telecom. Each machine on the local Ethernet was given an IP address. The Ethernet was connected to the Internet by a cisco gateway, which does all the routing

between the local Ethernet and the WWW server. The protocol TCP/IP runs over the ISDN connection, and the WWW server has a database of all the IP addresses of different LANs at schools in Hordaland.

The WWW server is called *gudmund*, after our former minister of education in Norway. The URL of this Web site is **http://gudmund.vgs.no**. *Gudmund* establishes the WWW service for the high schools in Hordaland and some primary schools from the Bergen community.

The way the schools in our region are connected to the Internet represents a centralized model. The *gudmund* server is a common resource for all the schools of this region. Several routines have been developed so that students from different schools can have an account on this machine. The server offers different Internet services to the various schools. This has many advantages. It means each

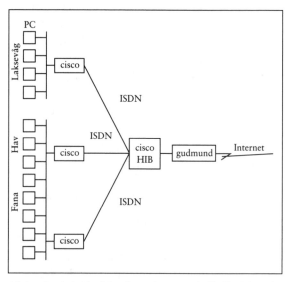

High schools in Hordaland county connected to the Internet by an ISDN connection.

school does not need to have very much knowledge of computer technology to administer its Internet connection. We hope to improve competence in computer science by building up a common resource server for all the schools. By using a powerful UNIX machine as a common WWW server for all the schools, one makes it easier from a technical point of view to administer their Internet services. The project has been going on for two years now and has been quite successful.

GUDMUNDSTAD

When the students at different schools in Hordaland connect to their accounts, they come into a "virtual city" called *gudmundstad*. In *gudmundstad* there are three main domains for getting information. There is one domain for *colleges*, one domain for *high schools*, and another domain for *primary schools*.

The Gudmundstad *city.*

When choosing the domain for the secondary schools, one gets a list of all the schools that are connected to *gudmund*. Many schools outside Hordaland county are also connected to the Internet in this way. If you click on one of the schools, you will get the *home page* of this school. You can then get some information about the school, when it was founded, how many teachers and students it has, and so on. At some schools the teachers have also developed their own home pages. In this way the particular teacher can present her- or himself, what subjects s/he is teaching, etc. Some students have also made their own home pages, where they write about themselves, what they are studying, and their hobbies.

From *gudmundstad* you can also send email to different places in Hordaland and to many other schools in our country. You can also get an overview of different newspapers and journals on many subjects, like the economy, computer science, social and natural science, and so on.

In another domain you can enter the *library service* of the secondary schools in Hordaland and elsewhere in Norway. You can be linked to many other secondary school libraries, BIBSYS (the library service of the universities and colleges in Norway), the national library service in Norway, and many other libraries in Norway and around the world connected to the Internet.

Gudmundstad as a Learning Environment

Gudmundstad has been used extensively in practical education. Of course, one such use has been in the school libraries, where school librarians undertake searches on particular subjects, or where schools gather information about various subjects, but more recently, schools have also developed home pages on a wide variety of subjects. Teachers have created HTML pages in subjects like history, geography, mathematics, etc., which they can use to exchange ideas.

One high school developed a project where four different countries collaborated to publish a newspaper electronically in four different languages. This project is called the *Interlingua* project.

Another high school started a project about Norse mythology. The students designed Web pages about the beliefs of the Vikings, and the project was nicely integrated in history lessons. Links were also established with schools in Scotland, a country that has much in common with Norway. It shares a similar geographical position and religious heritage, as well as having many isolated communities.

In our current treatment of history, there is an increasing emphasis on local and ordinary lives. This is a kind of history that cannot be easily read about in books, but by establishing contacts between students in different local communities via the Internet, we have seen how local history can be brought to life through the everyday details of peoples' lives, such as their names, the kind of work they do, the number of children they have, and so on.

Some primary schools in Bergen used *gudmundstad* to establish electronic contact with other students in Kobe, Japan, and Cape Town, South Africa. The students were informed about the developments in these countries and the fears and aspirations people have there. The opportunity to establish international contacts like these have become quite important now in the Norwegian curriculum.

We are beginning to see the implications of the technological changes that have taken place here in Norway and elsewhere in Europe. These will have profound consequences for new forms of learning, and for building an understanding of the importance of lifelong learning. The application of learning technologies in distance learning complements and enriches more conventional modes of education and training. In this connection we see *Gudmundstad* as a potential model for flexible and distance learning.

CHAPTER 19

Connected Information and Learning Communities: I*EARN, Global Art, and Learning Circles

by
Margaret Riel
Associate Director
Center for Collaborative Research in Education
University of California, Irvine

Title	I*EARN, Global Art and Learning Circles
Level	K–12
Type	Focus on information; interaction; task
Tool(s)	Email, listserv, Web
Contact	Margaret Riel mriel@iearn.org http://www.iearn.org

"The real power of telecommunications lies in its ability to bring people together," writes Margaret Riel, adding that it is really *"connected information"* and that *"Our print technologies make it possible to share our ideas. However, once recorded and reproduced, the links from author to reader, from artist to audience, from individual interest to a community of learners, are not a part of the product."*

In this chapter, Margaret describes the International Education and Resource Network, *or I*EARN, which uses international communications technologies to enable young people to undertake projects "designed to make a meaningful contribution to the health and welfare of the planet and its people."*

She focuses primarily on two examples: Global Art and Human Warmth, *and the highly regarded* Learning Circles *program, which she created. Students and teachers at all levels who share I*EARN's commitment to "youth making a difference in the world through telecommunications" will benefit from Margaret's practical thoughts and project guidelines, and they will appreciate her view that the work undertaken in these projects "celebrates and renews the human spirit."*

Many thanks to Margaret for describing her work here.

Communication Age

Telecommunication technologies are moving us from an information age to a communication age. The exciting changes taking place in education result from more extensive and stimulating "communities of learning." A community of learners is a group of people who value a specific set of information and skills.

INTERNATIONAL EDUCATION AND RESOURCE NETWORK (I*EARN)

The *International Education and Resource Network (I*EARN)* is an online global community of learners who share a concern for the physical and social health of our planet. Collective action is a powerful force and the I*EARN community helps students realize that they can use this power to make the planet a better place for all of us to live. Students, teachers, and a rich community of human and informational resources are joined and these connections shape a world view that celebrates learning in the service of others. Students working together in communities of learners have more power—individually and collectively—to participate in meaningful ways on local and world stages. I will give two examples, one drawn from the *Global Art* project and the second from team-teaching and learning in *Global Learning Circles*.

Global Art and Human Warmth

The I*EARN community has sponsored a number of Global Art exchanges, including A Sense of Family, Habitats: A Sense of Places, Indigenous People's Art Project, and a photo essay exchange called Olympics in My Community. The images are as beautiful as any found in art books that feature youth artists from different countries. However, these online images retain their connections to the student community that created them. The following story illustrates the power of this "connected information."

For the Indigenous People's Art Project, schools in Hungary, Thailand, Australia, and the U.S. exchanged artwork as well as video clips and email messages. Siriluck Hiri-O-tapa from the International School in Bangkok traveled to the village of the indigenous Karen tribe to include their participation. She showed the dormitory at the Baan Nu-Se-Plo School on a video clip sent to the other schools. She explained how the structure is drafty and cold and the students sleep without blankets. Students in the other countries responded in the way many do when a problem has human dimensions, they decided to help.

The students from A. Shiwi Elementary School in Zuni, New Mexico, made 400 greeting cards with original blanket designs, and sold the cards for a $1 each, raising $400. Students at the Bairnsdale Secondary School in Australia held a "Sausage Sizzle" to raise money as well. The students earned enough money to pay for blankets and a new power generator. These students wanted to share their warmth with their art partners. The teachers from these classes will be a part of a worldwide annual I*EARN community meeting. They will bring more messages and pictures from the students who were engaged in this effort to share resources with their art community.

PROJECT DESIGN

Designing around an issue or theme is one way to create learning communities. I*EARN teachers have created dozens of projects that invited participation by other classes. Some involve collaborative publishing while others organize science investigations, social action, and service learning.

Learning Circles: Teamwork on Projects

Participation in a Learning Circle also forms communities of learners. Learning Circles are groups of about eight classes from schools across the globe. The classes come from the same curriculum area and agree to work as partners helping each other learn. Instead of everyone working on a single project, each class has the opportunity to "sponsor" a project. These are often drawn from or related to classroom lessons. There is a reciprocal responsibility to participate in all of the projects in the Circle.

The Circle begins with activities designed to help teachers and students meet their peers and learn basic information about their schools and communities. One of these activities involves mailing such materials to participating schools for bulletin board displays. The materials exchanged allow students to understand the similarities and differences between one another's schools and countries.

In the next phase each of the schools introduces a project. Teachers often divide their students into groups and have each group take responsibility for their participation in one of the Circle projects. In this arrangement the teachers and students have the opportunity to learn from their work on different tasks. Teachers get a chance to see how their colleagues in other countries create lessons or projects. They are also able to watch their students work on a project organized by a distant teacher and student group.

Each class has the support and direction to create an online project within a general theme. Examples of projects from a high-school Mind Works Circle, centered around the theme of creative writing, include requests for descriptions of the best and worst teacher, stories that involve brothers or sisters, parent-teenager conflicts, surveys of how students spend time outside of school, and attitudes about drug use and violence.

In a Places and Perspective Learning Circle, centered around the theme of history and geography, student projects include: designing historical visits to one's city; writing letters or journal entries from the perspective of a person who lived in the locale in a different era or during a critical period of history; profiling local heroes, or interviewing community leaders. Learning Circle projects bring kids out into their community and help them understand how it resembles and differs from those in other regions and countries.

As in the example of the art project, it is often the work that takes place around the projects that is the most interesting part of Circle interaction. Students and teachers become interested in news events that take place in their partners' countries. Elections, disasters, accomplishments, wars, weather extremes, suicides, and

LEARNING CIRCLES ON I*EARN

Learning Circles are interactive, project-based partnerships among a small number of classes in schools located throughout the world. There are two sessions each year: September to January, and February to May. Each session is fourteen weeks long. To join a Learning Circle, you must be a member of I*EARN and complete a Learning Circle placement form two weeks before the beginning of the session. The I*EARN Web site is: **www.iearn.org**

SAMPLE LEARNING CIRCLE TIMELINE

Getting Ready—Prior to Week One
Teachers log on to I*EARN, receive Circle News, and read the Teacher's Guide. They introduce the concept of Learning Circles to their students.

Opening the Circle—Weeks One to Two
Learning Circle interaction begins. Classes log on and respond to the electronic roll call. Each teacher sends an introductory message to the online Learning Circle conference. Teachers and students prepare and send their responses to a Classroom Survey. Welcome Packs are mailed to postal addresses.

Planning the Learning Circle Projects—Weeks Three to Four
Teachers in the Learning Circle discuss the projects proposed in the Classroom Survey. Each class selects a section to sponsor. The class sends a message to the conference describing the information it would like to receive.

Exchanging Student Work—Weeks Five to Ten
Student work on different projects is collected and sent to the Learning Circle conference at least once or twice a week. Teachers and students continue to plan and share work related to the Learning Circle. (Most groups will be out of school for at least a week during this period, but the Circle continues with those who are in school.)

Organizing the Circle Publication—Weeks Eleven to Twelve
Students evaluate, select, and edit the articles they received for their project. Teachers work with students in their classroom to lay out and print their section of the Circle publication. Schools exchange project reports (electronically or via postal mail) and assemble their Circle publication.

Closing the Circle—Week Fourteen
Teachers and students send their final goodbye messages to the conference and the Learning Circle closes. The Christmas break is used as a time for mailing sections to the schools; the final comments and goodbyes take place when many students return to school in January. The list is still active for a week after the end of the Learning Circle to make sure all final messages are received.

social events become more interesting when one is connected to the people who are experiencing them. And because the students serve as informants to others, they must follow local events attentively.

The teachers also find that peers in other countries are valuable resources for new ideas or different perspectives. A teacher who is assessing portfolios and is struggling with a student graffiti problem, or who has to purchase new software, often finds that his or her peers in the Learning Circle can provide advice. Teachers share information directly or find a colleague at their school who has dealt with the problem or has special expertise. These kinds of "team-teaching" partnerships help isolated teachers become members of learning communities. When both teachers and students take time to reflect on the things that are happening in their lives, they provide others with a window into the many different ways of viewing life.

In times when Learning Circles partners have been caught by disasters—floods, earthquakes, and school fires—the people in their Learning Circle have come to the rescue in much the same way as students in New Mexico and Australia helped those in Thailand. They have sent books, learning materials, care packages, and messages of encouragement to those in distress.

CONNECTIONS AND COMMUNITIES

Students and teachers have been isolated in classrooms. At the turn of the century this isolation protected students from the abuses of the workplace. But these protective walls also isolated them from making meaningful contributions to the world they live in. Technology creates the bridge, but it is the community building that gives learning new life and life new meaning. Participation in learning communities like those made available by I*EARN helps students understand that their actions are valuable and that collective action can shape the world. Their work celebrates and renews the human spirit.

GLOBAL PROJECTS AND LEARNING CIRCLES ON I*EARN

I*EARN CREATIVE & LANGUAGE ARTS PROJECTS

Habitats Global Art Exchange
The Vision Literary Anthology
Photographic Exhibit: Olympics in My Community—Joint with Kodak
First People Art Project
Lewin Student Anthology

I*EARN SCIENCE/ENVIRONMENT PROJECTS

International Water Monitoring Project
Planetary Notions Environmental Newsletter
The Power of Math
Youth Can Environmental Action Project
Amazon to Antarctica Scientific Exploration

I*EARN SOCIAL STUDIES PROJECTS

The Comtemporary Global Newsmagazine
First Byte Project
Cultural Bridges with China
Faces of War
First/Indigenous Peoples
The Holocaust/Genocide Project
Inside View—An Urban Student Newsletter
Kids Can Elementary/Middle School Newsletter
Eradication of Poverty
World Religions Project
One Day in the Life Cross-Cultural Comparison
Clean Water for Nicaragua
Recovery/Substance Abuse
Stop Violence Project
World Millennium Project
E-Mail As Reconciliation Tool in Communities in Conflict
International Foods & Cultural Patterns

LEARNING CIRCLES

Circle Themes:
Places and Perspectives
Computer Chronicles
Mind Works
Learning Circles is available from the I*EARN web site.

CHAPTER 20

Learning to Do: Delivering Services and Developing Projects with ITM and Studio A

by
John Willinsky
Professor, Faculty of Education
University of British Columbia
Vancouver, British Columbia

Title	Learning to Do: Delivering Services and Developing Projects with ITM and Studio A
Level	Secondary
Type	Focus on technology; task
Tool(s)	Web
Contact	John Willinsky willinsk@unixg.ubc.ca http://www.knowarch.com

"Management is not about some individual who sits in the corner office," notes John Willinsky, *"but rather about individual and shared responsibility for getting the job done."*

That's the thinking behind the Information Technology Management (ITM) program, *which is based on John's work about learning in workplace settings, and how communications technologies can integrate work- and school-based learning.*

ITM is designed to provide secondary school students (e.g., grades ten to twelve) with skills and problem-solving abilities that are required in technology environments, both in industry and in post-secondary education. It is also designed to combine technical content with in-school work experiences in a curriculum that explores social and workplace issues associated with information technology.

One of the features of the program is Studio A, an online mentoring component, that is facilitated by industry partners drawn from the information technology sector. The mentors work with the students and teachers, blending sound business management strategies with sound classroom practice. In fact, the ITM curriculum was designed and developed in consultation with industry to ensure its relevance, and with secondary and post-secondary educators to ensure it meets existing standards in education.

We like the ways in which ITM draws on the strengths of industry and education in order to provide students with marketable skills in ways that both nurture and depend upon learning. One of the questions John poses, "What does it mean to learn through service to others?" underscores the fact that ITM was designed to enhance learning through authentic experiences.

It is "learning through the service of others" that actually sustains these experiences, and there are many contexts in which to act on your intentions to learn in this way. You will find a number of similarities between the ideas at the heart of ITM, a program that focuses on business, and those at the heart of I*EARN projects (pages 143–48), which focus on concerns of the "social and physical health" of our environment.

It is also worth noting that ITM reaches across many areas of interest, a number of which have examples here in the "Learning through Projects" section of The Learning Highway. The design and implementation of a school Web site, for instance, might well provide the impetus for involvement in projects like the Canadian Home Page Olympics (pages 118–21). And the notion of "shared responsibility" advanced here is also reflected in school-based projects like Dramapolooza (pages 127–31), national projects like KIDS FROM KANATA (pages 155–58) or WIER (pages 188–93), and in international projects like Learning Circles (pages 143–48).

In the ITM program, then, students can get involved in maintaining and developing technology systems in secondary schools, or in the curricular uses of educational technologies within schools. However, the foundation for learning—in ITM, and in other projects in this section—is the idea that that learning can happen through the service of others and by sharing expertise.

Our thanks to John for sharing his with us.

The Information Technology Management Program

"This course isn't about technology—it's about management!" declared a student in an exasperated but knowing tone of voice. The student was participating in a classroom debate about the upcoming year's learning outcomes for the Information Technology Management (ITM) course, which a high-school teacher was holding with her students. The student had come to recognize that learning how to manage technology is the key to ITM, and that management is not about some individual who sits in the corner office, but rather about individual and shared responsibility for getting the job done. The story also illustrates the collaboration of student and teacher that happens in an ITM course, where learning outcomes are met through the identification of personal, group, and "client" objectives, realized through a project-driven approach to studying information technology (IT) or computer studies for secondary school students (grades ten to twelve in Canada).

"M" IS FOR...
The defining characteristic of the ITM program is the M for management. The students learn to apply their skills to help others in the school

and community with new technologies; they provide this service through collaborative projects that enable them to learn and practice project management strategies commonly used in a knowledge economy. The students gain course credit by providing technical support, training, software development, and communication of IT issues and opportunities, making the school's IT environment a better place for both learning and information management. As they do so, they examine the social issues surrounding information technology, whether these involve privacy, piracy, access, or gender. They come to see *managing* technology as a service they can provide to others, a service through which they learn more about people and work processes than just about technology. Providing technology services and participating in collaborative projects enables the students and teachers, as well as people in the community, to realize the potential of technology for learning, creating, sharing, and connecting.

What does it mean to learn through service to others? The ITM program is designed to provide students with authentic problem-solving experiences; they engage with different experts as they seek answers to technology challenges encountered while supporting users who need help. The program places the students in situations that develop their sense of accountability and responsibility. They learn about the nature of work in today's new economy, which is fueled by new technologies, where success is determined not by the ability to "build a better mousetrap," but by exemplary service to the customer. In British Columbia the services that students provide as part of the ITM program have been recognized as a form of accredited "work experience,"

which is required for graduation.

What do the students do in an ITM course? Well, here's an example of a project a student might take on. This example was sent to us by Laurane Parris, who teaches the program in a B.C. school. She writes that, "with this emphasis on helping people manage, ITM students offer services ranging from providing on-the-spot relief to such calls as 'Help, the printer's jammed!' or 'How do I send email?'" They also get deeply involved in more complex, longer term projects such as...

- Building a school home page that will go up this year on the Web.

- Creating animations in 3-D to run on the hall monitors displaying school/community events.

- Participating in the planning, configuring, and installation of a LAN at the nearby elementary school.

- Developing a presentation using HyperCard about peer counselors to guide students.

- Implementing a FirstClass server as the school's email system and bulletin board.

- Assembling a demonstration computer in a clear plastic case.

- Implementing a Web server to create and maintain Web pages for non-profit groups in the community.

- Planning a Web radio station for the broadcasting class to run.

- Establishing a production center for desktop publishing and multi-media presentations in the school.

SHARED EXPERTISE

Laurane points out that service involves the sharing of expertise. Every student in the class must teach, starting one to one and working toward full-scale presentations using PowerPoint to an audience of adults who are unfamiliar with the program. Students teach each other technical skills. They also teach the teachers. They give in-school workshops on the software used for grading, and according to Laurane, "by the end of term students who know ReMark are chased down hallways by desperate teachers." The students have also taught workshops to teachers on CorelDraw and have provided district Internet training where they were responsible for working with the librarian to train up to 1,400 students and 100 teachers.

And judging by the comments of the grade ten student who led the CorelDraw workshop, it was an exhilarating experience: "It was about November. Miss Jones just handed me this CorelDraw booklet and said, 'Learn the program.' I'd never used it before, never touched it. [She said,] 'Learn it because in two months you've got to teach a seminar on it to teachers,' and I was just like, 'I can't do this,' you know. And then when I came out of it, I taught the whole thing, and...no negative comments came back... Oh, it was a total, a total great achievement."

AWAY FROM THE SCREEN

One important aspect of ITM is its ability to draw students with an affinity for technology away from the screen and into sharing their expertise with others. This gives them a new set of skills and a sense of accomplishment. Working with people also has an appeal for

those students who have not traditionally been drawn to computer courses, such as young women. One young woman in the grade ten class explained it this way: "As I got into Information Technology Management, it seemed to be more girls, actually.... The boys seemed to be more attracted to it [initially] for some reason. That's why I was surprised that it seemed to be more girls, maybe because of the independence thing."

When it came to describing what she liked about the program, this student told us about the responsibility, independence, and sense of completeness she got from the work she did. "I think learning more about how to develop your own type of program which you're interested in... like I did for the Counseling Centre, that was the most positive thing, because I had to do the whole thing all together, instead of just learning about one thing one day and then changing to another one."

The Information Technology Management program was initiated in 1994 by Knowledge Architecture, a Vancouver company I established with Vivian Forsman, an IT industry professional. We founded the company to make a distinct social and technological contribution to Canada's telecommunications, information, and education infrastructure. The company worked with teachers and industry people to develop one of the first project-learning programs. Students have taken ITM courses in several Canadian provinces, and there have been discussions with a number of school districts in the U.S. as well.

STUDIO A

In its first year, ITM was offered as a traditional paper-based curriculum of learning outcomes and assessment activities. It was delivered by staff mentors who had experience in the IT industry and who visited the schools to show teachers and students how to provide a professional level of service to the school and community. This support is now delivered through a Web-based learning resource known as *Studio A*, which provides a workspace for each ITM student. Studio A forms a password-protected intranet—a local area network that conforms to Internet standards—within the ITM classroom for teachers and students, as well as a larger intranet among all of the ITM students in Canada and the U.S.

The student's personalized workspace has at its center a project book that provides the student with the templates, tables, and informational links needed to plan projects in collaboration with other students. The project book encourages students to achieve a high degree of accountability to both the "client" and the teacher. Students also have a set of electronic project tools they can access from their workspace to assist them with making presentations or Web pages or collaborating electronically. They also have an electronic portfolio in which to place materials to be evaluated by the teacher or to show to prospective employers.

We have learned from other service learning projects how critical it is to have students reflect on what they have accomplished through their projects and how they can grow. To facilitate this process, the student's project book includes a skills matrix where students can set goals and review their progress. The student can also reach out through the project book to telementors who have joined the ITM program to provide online help with technical and service questions, as well as career advice.

After working in their project books, students can also take a "virtual stroll" through the Studio A neighborhood, which offers them a chance to see what others in the program are up to in the Student Showcase. They can also visit the Café to get up-to-the-minute news and to exchange opinions, or seek or offer help. They can use the ThinkTank to evaluate issues and policies in essays or reports, or look up Just-in-Time-Learning to help them build the technical know-how they need for projects.

While ITM students are provided with a fully supported workspace on the Web, the ITM teacher is not forgotten. The teacher also has a personalized project book in Studio A, which serves as a management tool for the ITM class. Teachers can publish the course outline and requirements in all of the students' project books. They are able to track the students' projects, and evaluate and comment on the work that students place in their portfolio. They can use their project book to review the class's progress with students and parents. The Just-in-Time Learning section contains a special section about professional development for the teacher, which suggests how to teach in an ITM program based on other teachers' experiences. It also introduces teachers and students to professional methods used to deliver service in the IT industry.

After three years of developing the ITM program and building Studio A to support it, we are now expanding this Web-supported collaborative environment to include a wider range of subject areas. There's no limit to the projects and services students can get involved in. For example, they could provide marketing support to local businesses in business education classes; produce brochures for community groups in communications classes; or put on a play series in a drama class.

We'll give the final word to Laurane, who has been teaching in the ITM program during the last three years and manages to capture the excitement and challenge of traveling along the new learning highway:

Experience has convinced me that helping "clients" with real problems, teaching people about Web pages, or just being there on a help-desk is the most powerful motivator in the world, for students. Mind you, the other side of that is that being recognized as an expert can be pretty heady stuff at sixteen or seventeen. And part of your role as teacher is going to be helping students cope with these new roles and responsibilities.

CHAPTER 21

KIDS FROM KANATA and the Cradleboard Teaching Project

by Jonn Ord
Director, KIDS FROM KANATA
339 Wellesley St. E.
Toronto, Ontario

Title	KIDS FROM KANATA and the Cradleboard Teaching Project
Level	Middle School, Secondary, Post Secondary, Teacher Education
Type	Focus on information; interaction; task
Tool(s)	Computer-conferencing, Web
Contact	Jonn Ord kfk@scilink.org http://www.edu.yorku.ca/~KFK

KIDS FROM KANATA, *a project that links First Nations communities with other communities, operates in a* computer-conferencing *environment. This means that participants connect to a host system in order to participate in a discussion with others on a particular topic. Conferencing systems differ from other forms of computer-based group discussion, such as an* Internet newsgroup, *for example, in a few key ways.*

COMPUTER CONFERENCING

First, conferencing systems are usually operated by organizations that have a particular focus. Participants are people who have accounts on the particular conferencing system operated by that organization. In many cases, schools operate or have access to a local conferencing system or bulletin board system *(BBS).*

Second, unlike newsgroups, which are generally available to all Internet users, conferencing systems usually provide participants with access to discussions that may be open to everyone with an account or closed to participants in a specific project.

While this project will interest secondary-level students, we want to point out that KIDS FROM KANATA was initially developed for elementary school pupils. This is an important point because it demonstrates that the online skills you learn at one level may well be transferable to your work at other levels. Imagine, for instance, how students who used the KANATA project in elementary school might be using the Internet for learning as they grow through the school system.

Many thanks to Jonn Ord for telling us about this project.

KIDS FROM KANATA

OVERVIEW

KIDS FROM KANATA is a project that uses modern technology to connect First Nations students with students in mainstream schools across Canada. The project uses the highly-rated Canadian bulletin-board/conferencing software called FirstClass, accessible over the Internet, to create "virtual classrooms." To keep the exchanges personal and manageable, schools are linked together in triads consisting of one First Nations school and two mainstream schools. (The schools are usually in different provinces and often have very different geography, climates, and cultures.) A First Nations school becomes the host for each triad and students from that school name the triad with a significant word from their own language.

PIQATI TRIAD

Hi my name is Susie Aliqatuqtuq. I live in Broughton Island. Broughton Island is 120 km above the Arctic Circle. In my family I live with my dad and my mom and 2 brothers.

My Hobbies are ski-dooing and Babysitting and visiting my friends. My Best friend is Ina Allurut. I have 2 grammas, 1 grandpa. My dad's dad died when I was 4 years old. In spring time we go hunting for seal pup. We go fishing in June and July and also Berry picking in August and September on my grandpa's boat. My favorite show is Family Matters. After school I go home and clean up the house. My favorite sport is SOCCER.

During the course of the project, personal exchanges take place among those in a great range of circumstances:

There is violence in my community which is called Shamattawa Where I am originally from. I am willing to write about it because I know someone is going to listen, and I will do the same.

All my life I've seen violence, where people were getting beaten for no reason, when they can't get something done they beat the heck out of someone else. And its not just that abuse going around there is also emotional abuse and sexual abuse.

Well, I'm hoping deep in my heart that everything and everybody will be changed into something good so that the crys could be stopped.

I can't even stand to hear a baby or anyone else cry cause it hurts me, cause I know how they feel and I have been through it before. So if there is anything I can do I'll try hard to help …

Sincerely,
mary—**Beedabun School**

The heart of the program is a child-centered, interactive exploration of cultures, in particular First Nations culture. The project becomes a personal experience of discovery for each student and builds on our natural curiosity and desire to learn about ourselves and our friends.

The project leads students on an examination of Self and Family, Self and Community, Self and Society, Self in Location (geography), Self in the Context of History. Students progress from preliminary meetings and orientations to in-depth investigations of all three sites in their triad, by sharing information about themselves, their families, and their communities using Internet-based computer communications.

PROJECT BENEFITS

Personal relationships are formed among students at each of the partner schools and students are encouraged to maintain these relationships by establishing their own ID on the system and communicating directly with students at their partner locations throughout the program. Participants develop important computer and communication skills and through a largely self-directed research process find out a great deal about Canada that they would otherwise not have known. The project then allows the students to use this base of knowledge to create and refine responses to key issues for their own communities, such as unemployment, substance abuse, city crime. Most important, it offers them the possibility of taking action on these issues. As such, it engages students in a process of self-directed learning in which language, culture, and community are honored and respected as the letter (page 158) to Chief Ovide Mercredi from students at Lawrence Heights Middle School in North York, Ontario, indicates.

TEACHER EDUCATION

In the 1996–97 school year the KIDS FROM KANATA project was moved to the Faculty of Education at York University in Toronto. This resulted in a collaboration with the faculty and with the teacher candidates (TCs) in training at the faculty. A pair of TCs was assigned to each triad and supported the classroom teachers who were working on the project and facilitat-

ing the student discussions and exchanges on the system. This provided an innovative "virtual practicum" for the teacher candidates, enabling them to visit, on a regular basis, three remote classrooms, each in a different region of Canada. At the same time the young teachers learned a great deal about the Internet, online communications for distance education, and the behind-the-scenes operation of a large, national telecommunications program.

This collaboration was so successful that we are planning to increase the involvement of the TCs so that each classroom teacher will now be assigned a "dedicated" teacher candidate. As well, the TCs will receive extra training about the use of the system, moderating techniques, and other useful Internet skills.

The Cradleboard Teaching Project

Another exciting project involves our long-time sponsor and friend, Buffy Sainte-Marie. Buffy has been working hard developing the Cradleboard Teaching Project in the U.S., linking up Native American schools with mainstream U.S. schools and developing innovative tribally based curriculum. The program start-up was funded by the W.K. Kellogg Foundation.

Buffy has invited KANATA staff members to collaborate with the Cradleboard team and to make a contribution to the project, based on our experience of working on the Canadian program.

The Cradleboard pilot is using the same FirstClass software to connect the schools over the Internet for the interactive part of the project and is currently sharing the FirstClass server

Dear Chief Mercredi,

We read your letter and we're happy to see that you had time to write to us. We studied about Native Peoples when we were in grade 7 and ever since, our feelings have changed and we have developed a great respect for the Native Peoples. The study has helped us become more open minded, more understanding, and more tolerant. We would now like to share with you the parting words of our project.

When will the struggle ever end? We talk about world hunger, but we have beggars on our own streets. We talk about Canada, place of freedom and equality, but we do not listen to our First Peoples. Our government talks about multiculturalism, but who did the most harm to the Natives Peoples? The government, of course.

We are Canadians; we are red blooded human beings. When are we ever going to live up to our promises? Those same promises we made to the Native People have come back to haunt us. It is time to admit our mistakes to ourselves. We cannot change the fact that we have scared the Native Peoples. We cannot change the fact that we have scared ourselves in the process too but we have a chance to make a difference today. Here. Now the future is up to all of us to shape, young and old.

Now for the big question. To whom does the land belong? No one person can own the land. None of us can say that the world belongs to us because none of us can answer all the questions and solve the mysteries of the world. You and I are just a part of the Earth. We belong to the Earth. The Earth does not belong to us. Our project has helped us to become more aware of just some of the many problems in Canada. We feel it is time for all of us to come together as one and face our problems together, to create a better future.

Sincerely,
Chan Phothirath, Ashu Singh

located at the Faculty of Education at York. While the Cradleboard and KIDS FROM KANATA project members cannot "see" each other's projects, some students and teachers from both projects have informally "met" each other online and participated in casual online chats.

Project directors Jonn Ord and Buffy Sainte-Marie hope that one day their programs will work together more directly. It has always been a goal to make the KIDS FROM KANATA project truly bi-cultural in its operation as well as in its content and membership.

Meanwhile the projects continue to support each other as they develop their separate operating personalities. The Cradleboard project has a mandate to develop and deliver innovative Native curriculum to the classroom in addition to the interactive online part of the program. Cradleboard is also hoping to develop a close relationship with the U.S. Tribal Colleges, operated by the American Indian Higher Education Consortium (AIHEC) and to involve student teachers in curriculum implementation and project support.

CHAPTER 22

Kids as Global Scientists

by
Nancy Butler Songer, Project Director
Holly Devaul, Project Manager
School of Education, University of Michigan
Ann Arbor, Michigan

Title	Kids as Global Scientists
Level	Secondary
Type	Focus on interaction
Tool(s)	Email, message boards, Web
Contact	Holly Devaul onesky@umich.edu http://onesky.engin.umich.edu

The Kids as Global Scientists (KGS) *project combines a number of possible Internet experiences—including access to scientific information and interaction with online mentors—with field-based research experiences, which are undertaken offline at local sites. It can be undertaken in ways that use many Internet resources and tools, and we think you will find the integrated approaches taken here quite useful.*

Another excellent element of KGS is that it shows how Internet skills are transferable. As you will see, it began as a project focused at the middle school level, but it now operates at elementary- through secondary-school levels.

Nancy and Holly wish to thank Janet Carlson Powell for her thoughtful review of this chapter, and we wish to thank them all for their contribution to this book.

KGS began in 1992, with a grant from the National Science Foundation. The principal investigator is Dr. Nancy Butler Songer, Assistant Professor at the University of Colorado's School of Education and Institute of Cognitive Science. Additional support was conferred in 1995 when Dr. Songer was presented with an NSF Presidential Faculty Fellowship and a Networking Infrastructure for Education (NIE/NSF) grant to continue and expand the project.

ATMOSPHERIC SCIENCE
The KGS research group has developed an Internet and Web-enhanced curricula designed to encourage middle-school student inquiry and research about concepts in atmospheric science. Students use visualization and telecommunica-

tion technologies to learn about these concepts both locally and through interactions with peers and resources worldwide. In conjunction with this, KGS conducts research into student learning and motivation and a variety of issues related to integrating technology into the classroom. Project materials and staff can be reached at our web site, or via email.

The original KGS curriculum is an eight-week general weather unit. It follows a "progressive constructivist" approach to learning as it strives to maximize the educational potential of a network-based middle school curriculum. This approach is one in which students "construct" or build their own knowledge and understanding by exploring concepts on their own or through guided activities, rather than being presented with a set of facts. For example, students collect their own weather data, such as temperature and pressure, wind speed and direction, and cloud type, and conduct tests for acid rain or snow. Local understandings are then enhanced and expanded using the Internet and its resources, which include correspondence with peers and meteorologists worldwide, the sharing of student-collected data, and real-time and archival satellite and weather imagery. The curriculum also includes suggestions for hands-on classroom experiments and demonstrations, interdisciplinary activities exploring weather folklore, and writing for an online newspaper.

Since its inception, Kids as Global Scientists has grown considerably. We continue to research ways to scale the program to larger numbers allowing us to offer this type of learning experience to an ever greater range of students. With each passing year, the number of participants

has increased, from six schools in the first year, to approximately eighty schools and four thousand students in 1997. Participants have included students, teachers, and scientists from across the United States as well as from Australia, Brazil, Canada, Hong Kong, Finland, Scotland, South Africa, Guam, Spain, and Romania. In the past year we have accepted students from a greater range of ages, and have increased the diversity of settings to include home-schools, rural schools, and alternative schools, as well as urban and suburban sites.

In addition to expanding participation, in 1996 we began work on a series of curricula as part of our research collaboration with the University of Michigan's Weather Underground. These programs will be shorter in duration (four weeks) and will focus on specific weather or environmental phenomena, such as hurricanes and water quality. These units will continue to emphasize hands-on learning; students will explore the topics through a variety of guided activities using the resources available on the Web. Our first program, titled One Sky, Many Voices: Hurricanes '96, was timed to coincide with the hurricane season in the northern hemisphere. This curriculum was our first venture into developing Web-based activities and discussion groups, or message boards, for communication between students and scientists.

Adopt-a-Hurricane
The University of Michigan provides technical expertise in designing imagery, data files, and text-based forecasts to be used in conjunction with this project. This interface allows students to track hurricanes as they happen, as well as review predictions about the paths and data of

previous storms. Presenting the hurricane data in multiple ways (graphically, numerically, and textually) is a key part of the learning approach in our work, allowing students a variety of paths to construct their own understandings of the phenomena of hurricanes. For example, the Adopt-a-Hurricane activity encourages students to interact with content specialists as they follow the life history of a current storm, comparing the predictions with the reality as it plays itself out. The sensational nature of hurricanes is fascinating for many students and can provide strong motivation for learning. However we also include activities and first-hand reports that reveal the devastating effect these phenomena can have on humans and the coastline.

New efforts in 1997 include an exploration into the WebTV interface, and the development of companion projects, with both formal classroom and informal, at-home participation options. Topics include Severe Storms, Water Quality, Endangered Species, Science for Girls, and Air Quality. All these projects will continue to emphasize hands-on learning experiences in which students can explore ideas in a variety of ways. They will also each have a mechanism for online discussion and data sharing, and will utilize Internet technology for access to real-time data as well as the multitude of visual resources that the Web offers. Information about these projects will be at **http://onesky.engin.umich.edu** as they develop.

EDUCATIONAL RESEARCH

In addition to developing curriculum we are simultaneously conducting educational research in a number of areas. For example, we are exploring the idea that the learning environment provided by the KGS units may benefit groups of students who do not thrive in a traditional classroom setting, or for whom science has become an intimidating topic.

Online and Classroom Settings

We are particularly interested in the ways that incorporating technology into the curriculum might empower such students. Teachers have shared with us stories of students whose frustration and lack of self-esteem prevented them from participating in class. In some cases finding the freedom to express themselves in an email message triggered a complete change in the students' achievement.

Teacher Deann Bucher writes about a significant and encouraging turnaround in one of her most challenging students:

> Academically, Gwen (not her real name) has two qualities that influence her. The first is that she has a real desire to be successful. This desire to learn and to do well frequently brings her to tears of frustration. The second factor that influences Gwen is a learning disability. Gwen has continually been given the message from both the school and her family that she is inferior.
>
> But fortunately, this is the Gwen of the past. This endless pattern of frustration and despair has ended. The key to ending this cycle has been the use of Internet technology in her classroom. During the spring of 1995, Gwen participated in the Kids as Global Scientists project in order to study weather. Gwen was very excited about communicating with other students during the project. In a short, forty-minute period, her academic life took on new meaning. She was no longer filling blank spaces on a page with meaningless and diffi-

cult words. Instead, she was communicating with other students around the world.

As a teacher, I never knew that Gwen could spell, format coherent sentences, and use proper grammar. I will never forget the first, proud paragraph of her letter: "Hi. I'm Gwen Romero!" While to some observers, this may not have been an appropriate introduction for this type of letter, it proclaimed for the first time an image of a girl who was not hiding, but was proud to say "Hello, World. I am here." The Internet became a source of constant interest for Gwen. She asked daily to use the computer lab, and sent out a number of letters that demonstrated her writing abilities as they had never shown before.

Learning Science and Teacher Education

Another research focus has been how the use of a curriculum like KGS might change and influence both the nature of students' understanding of science as well as teacher practices. Exposure to and interaction with real-time data, peers, and professionals can change the types of understanding that students develop compared with traditional library-centered or locally-based investigations. Integrating personal experiences and a wider array of resources into the student's understanding of a concept creates a broader base of knowledge and can personalize the science. In addition, learning that involves information-gathering via the Internet can foster a sense of independence and ownership for students. This can present challenges to the teacher, both in terms of classroom management and in developing ways to integrate these resources into students' work as a whole. We encourage our teachers to have students create portfolios as a final product of their participation in KGS. These pieces of work can vary considerably, but allow the students to synthesize their body of work, finding the connections between what they have gleaned from Internet resources, hands-on activities, online mentors, local data collection and traditional library research. Making connections between their work and the resources on the Internet enhances their local observations and frames these observations in a larger perspective. KGS teachers report that giving their students a sense of ownership, as well as finding ways to use Internet technology to relate to students' personal lives, is a key factor in the success of these programs. The challenge before us is to create a learning environment in which the Internet is not just a provider of facts but also stimulates students to formulate their own questions and then to use the technology to answer those questions.

Learning from Students

Learning in this way can also change a teacher's role in the classroom from lecturer or provider of information to facilitator. This often requires a shift in perspective as well as changes in classroom management. We have discussed this with KGS teachers over the years and are now examining more formally how integrating technology into the classroom affects them, as well as how electronic communities might support their own professional development goals. These discussions are facilitated via an electronic listserv, which also provides a forum for teacher-to-teacher exchanges and the sharing of ideas. We feel these conversations will play a key role in the further development of our curricula and also contribute to the growing body of research about teaching practice.

CHAPTER 23

PHICYBER—"A Virtual Classroom: The Electronic Agora"

by
Ron Barnette, Professor and Head
Department of Philosophy
Valdosta State University
Valdosta, Georgia

Title	PHICYBER—"A Virtual Classroom: The Electronic Agora"
Level	Post Secondary
Type	Focus on information; task
Tool(s)	Listserv, Web
Contact	Ron Barnette rbarnett@valdosta.edu http://www.valdosta.edu/-~rbarnett/phi

In the last edition of The Learning Highway, *Dr. Ron Barnette considered how students in his* Philosophy in Cyberspace (PHICYBER) *program would regard one another when communication occurred through written texts rather than face-to-face. This issue surfaced before in this book when we noted how online*

"you are what you say you are" and how it is the textual nature of some programs that makes them successful. Programs like Writers in Electronic Residence operate this way, and we mention it now because of two points that emerge from Ron's update to his course at Valdosta State University in Valdosta, Georgia, U.S.A.

AN ONLINE RECORD

*First, he notes that all work done online for courses becomes "part of a record." This is an idea that is explored by Andrew Feenberg, a professor of philosophy at San Diego State University. Feenberg tells us that the kind of online "record" that Ron writes about is useful because it is "retrievable." * How many times have you wanted to replay a conversation, or wondered if you had said something a certain way in a conversation? To Feenberg, online communication is a kind of "written world," and in this world, some things—like communication—happen differently because they can be retrieved. This leads us to our second point.*

---

* Feenberg's article is on the Web at:
http://www-icdl.open.ac.uk/mindweave/mindweave.html

REFLECTION

Most of the time, when we speak to others, we do it "now," in "real time." Online, though, you have the opportunity to compose your thoughts. It is true, of course, that many people use online communication as a kind of "talking," and this is also reasonable. After all, you can simply reply to a message while you are online and use it in a conversational way, like talking on a telephone.

You do have another choice, though, and that is that you don't have to. Online, you can decide whether you want to respond at all, and if you do, whether to do so now or later. This presents you with options that may not be available in face-to-face situations, like a class, for example, and one of them is to see online communication as writing more than "talk." This presents the online learner with the opportunity to engage in a discussion with others, but in a way that lets you reflect on your thoughts, and compose your ideas to your satisfaction before offering a response, or starting a new idea.

Teaching on the Internet has changed Ron's role as a teacher. He now participates with his students in shared learning experiences rather than simply lecturing to them. Since 1994 his listserv-based project has evolved to incorporate the World Wide Web.

Many thanks to Ron for raising such intriguing questions in his update about PHICYBER.

As an educator and experimenter of sorts, in 1993 I contemplated offering at Valdosta State University a Special Topics in Philosophy course during the summer of 1994, to be conducted entirely through the computer. Using the Internet, how would a class, whose members know one another only through their thoughts written down and exchanged, differ from the standard context, where bodily presence is an integral part of communication and dialogue? How would library research projects fare in this medium, where online resources available through an electronic source would constitute the essential research infrastructure; where individual critiques would be prepared between classroom authors whose personal identities are shaped for others only by the written word; where "you are what you write"?

After discussion with colleagues and students, I decided to develop and conduct such a course. Titled "A Virtual Classroom: The Electronic Agora", the course is accessible online twenty-four hours a day, seven days a week, for the ten-week term. Twenty-one participants made up the class, with one in Texas, another in New York, one in Illinois and yet another in North Carolina, in addition to the remaining "on-campus" members. Since 1994, this course has been offered during summer terms at Valdosta State, and its growth has been remarkable. In 1996, 111 students signed up for the course from eleven countries representing five continents! Philosophical dialog and debate was now happening in a global multicultural environment, due entirely to computing information technology. Unique classroom experiences were now a reality, as students across the world discussed topics forged in the cyberspace community around the clock.

During the course all classroom discussion and

dialog is conducted through electronic mail, via a listserver, PHICYBER, to which all class members subscribe. Through our Valdosta State Philosophy Website (**http://www. valdosta.peachnet.edu/~rbarnett/phi**), an electronic academic department is available for the worldwide philosophy community, and PHICYBER members make use of the vast resources and materials available through, for example, our Virtual Library, an electronic doorway through which hundreds of philosophy works, journals, articles, and resources are available. These growing collections are in the Virtual Library thanks to links provided by the excellent philosophy Web sites around the globe, which are also available at our site. Indeed, collaboration and sharing are marvelous enablers, and it is thanks to the international philosophy community that such library reserves are now online. I have recently discovered, much to my pleasure, that philosophers (in and out of academe) and departments of philosophy have been in the forefront of making academic materials available through the Web. By means of these cost-free resources, PHICYBER students pursue their research and develop written projects and Web home pages around philosophical themes, all of which are submitted in electronic form. The Electronic Agora is totally paperless.

Regarding class discussion through the PHICYBER list, each week a topic and problem are assigned for discussion, accompanied by assigned readings and notes, which are also available through a PHICYBER home page at our Web site. As discussion progresses, it is remarkable to watch relationships unfold, based only, as agreed, upon one another's ideas, criticized and expanded. Members respond to the discussion topic, defend their positions, raise critical objections, respond to challenges, and reflect on implied new directions for analysis and further critical thought. As one student put it, "It is so different when you have to think through your ideas, put them in writing, and be prepared to back up your views, knowing that once expressed they are out there for the permanent record!" This student alludes to the fact that all classroom work and discussions are placed in a course archive and are available for ongoing retrieval and review. Think of the "in-class" portion of the course as a transcript. There are no voices or accents, no noises, or distractions based on gender, race, ethnicity, or age—only ideas, and ideas on ideas, formulated, written and rewritten, expressed, and revisited.

Through PHICYBER I have changed much of what I do as a teacher. No longer standing before a class, I now involve the students in course goings-on much more, as I participate with them in our shared electronic voyages. The interpersonal conduct is ethically respectful of each other's thoughts and deeds, and the level of learning indicates a richness not readily apparent in traditional settings. It is quite clear that our Electronic Agora is a wonderful classroom without walls! And I invite readers to pay a visit to PHICYBER, located off the Valdosta Philosophy Web site listed above. I am convinced that the electronic medium can provide unlimited opportunities for those whose personal situation marries well with the occasion. For example, disabled students' whose physical handicap might make it difficult for them to thrive in a traditional university setting can flourish in a virtual class-room. I am equally convinced that the "virtual classroom" model should be a supplement to existing university life. I am old-fashioned and wise enough to realize that face-to-face interactions are indispensable. After all, these occasions shape real-world involvement, even if such involvement is becoming more and more computer-mediated.

CHAPTER 24

From Email to Visualization

by
Aleš Čepek and Josef Hnojil
Department of Mapping and Cartography
Faculty of Civil Engineering
Czech Technical University
Prague, Czech Republic

Title	From Email to Visualization
Level	Post Secondary
Type	Focus on technology
Tool(s)	Email, programming languages, Web
Contact	Aleš Čepek and Josef Hnojil cepek@fsv.cvut.cz, hnojil@fsv.cvut.cz http://gama.fsv.cvut.cz/

In the first edition of The Learning Highway *(1995), teacher Aleš Čepek and student Josef Hnojil described their first experience with using the Internet in teaching and learning at the Czech Technical University (CTU) in Prague. This was not a simple matter. As they note, "In the Czech Republic we used to count our connection to the Internet in months at that time," and they began to describe their situation as follows:*

About a year ago I peeped for the first time into the world of computer networks. Within a couple of days I was able to enter the cyberspace of the Internet. All dreams of medieval alchemists, fumbling on their way to the philosophers' stone, fade when compared with the present reality of the Internet—a living ocean of information flowing through computer networks all over the world, lying at our fingertips and at our service.

My previous feelings, which were not in any case exceptional, were intensified by the simple fact that I was born in a country living its poor existence in a gloomy shadow of an Iron Curtain. The civilized world had a period of about twenty years to adopt the phenomenon of computer networks as an integral part of its culture. Our universities joined the European Academic & Research Network (EARN) *towards the end of 1990; our first link to Internet was around February 1992.*

Since my very first contacts with the Internet, I have been absolutely sure that it is essential for our students that I work to enable their access to the network and to introduce them to the field of networking. Therefore in the autumn of 1992, I included the Internet within the curriculum of a seminar entitled "Introduction to data-processing."

In this piece we want to present Aleš and Josef's ongoing projects, which involve the use of the Internet in the Department of Mapping and Cartography in the Faculty of Civil Engineering, Czech Technical University (CTU), Prague.

Many thanks to Aleš and Josef for updating us on their work. We will also hear from Josef in the last chapter, "What Students Say."

When we started teaching the Internet as a new subject we placed the most emphasis on technical aspects, describing and practicing using Internet services. At the same time, we worked on changing our curriculum to integrate the Internet into it. In a sense, this was simply a necessity because even today we cannot assume that secondary school graduates entering CTU will be familiar with the Internet, or its use to them in their studies.

At present all our students attend an introductory course focused on the Internet in the first year of their studies. They are supplied with Internet accounts that have full connectivity. In our course the emphasis is on participation in electronic conferences and the ability to use the information resources of the WWW.

In many respects, the role of the Internet in education represents an extraordinary phenomenon. The Internet can be a great motivation to students, stimulating personal initiatives. For some of our courses we run local conferences online, and our experience is that these conferences are a highly productive educational instrument. For example, in our conference on the C++ computer programming language, students are supposed to answer and solve the majority of queries. Active work in local conferences is also good practical training for future Internet work.

As soon as students in our course become familiar with the Internet, we shift our attention from tools to Internet resources and how to find them. Each student has to present a paper on a given topic. Students are free to choose their theme from a supplied list, with topics that range from technical or arts subjects to social problems. They are also invited to propose their own one. (We want to avoid a strictly technical point of view.) The paper has to be based on information obtained from the Internet.

The papers are posted online in a local conference, which is dedicated to our introductory course, for discussion. In addition to presenting his or her paper online, each student is expected to comment on and evaluate two other papers in the conference. In the conference the discussion is not limited to a study group but is open to all our students enrolled in the current year. Teachers act in the conference more or less as its moderators.

For those students who want to learn more

about Internet technologies we open a seminar in which among other topics we introduce them into system LINUX (a public domain clone of UNIX). There are several reasons why we have chosen LINUX.

- UNIX is still very important in scientific applications as well as in the remote sensing, geographical information systems, and digital photogrammetry—the fields our graduates work in.

- Basic knowledge of UNIX is needed in order to take advantage of the software facilities at the CTU super-computing center (**http://www.civ.cvut.cz**); e.g., parallel computing or scientific visualization.

- LINUX is an excellent platform for students to use to get a deeper understanding of lower levels of Internet technologies; our students' server GaMa (Geodesy and Mapping) (**http://gama.fsv.cvut.cz/**) is running under OS LINUX and is maintained by our students and Ph.D. students.

Other topics of the seminar are HTML (Hypertext Markup Language) and SGML (Standard Generalized Markup Language). SGML is a possible solution to various problems concerning textual information in geographic information systems. As a model SGML example, we present to our students the "LINUX Documentation Project," which defines a unified scheme for writing reports in SGML. The documents can be converted to HTML, ASCII, LaTeX, Postscript and other formats.

The most remarkable activity of our Ph.D. students (Jan Dousa and David Landspersky), in which selected students participate, is the project "*EUREF* Local Analysis Center GOP." The main task for *EUREF* (European Reference Frame) is the establishment, maintenance, and enhancement of a three-dimensional European Reference Frame. The project is a collaboration between the Geodetic Observatory "Pecny" and CTU Prague. It involves processing and analyzing large volumes of satellite data, collected from various Internet FTP servers. You can learn more about the project, which is supervised by Dr. Leos Mervart, at:

http://gama.fsv.cvut.cz/euref/

The last project we would like to describe deals with visualization in cartography, the subject of Josef's Ph.D. Scientific visualization is one of the tools for analyzing and processing large volumes of data. With our department's limited funds we cannot get the powerful hardware needed for the visualization. Nevertheless, a professional system is available online. The AVS (Advanced Visualization System) is installed at CTU's super-computing center (**http://www.civ.cvut.cz/**). We did not have all the background we needed, so we contacted Professor Alan M. MacEachren at Pennsylvania State University, who is the chairperson of the Commission on Visualisation of the International Cartography Association, asking him for help. Although the references he sent us in reply could probably be found using any good search engine on the Internet, a search engine would not have given us the personal contacts to other specialists in this field. For us, the means provided by the Internet for effective communication and collaboration like we had with Professor MacEachren is the most important contribution.

CHAPTER 25

Strong Women in Film

by
Winifred Wood
Director, the Writing Program
Wellesley College
Wellesley, Massachusetts

Title	Strong Women in Film
Level	Post Secondary
Type	Focus on information; interaction; task; technology
Tool(s)	Web
Contact	Winifred Wood wwood@wellesley.edu http://www.wellesley.edu/ Writing/Strongwomen/index.html

One of the things we really like about this project, which explores the introduction of the Web into a university course on women in film, is how the relationships between class members changed when students used the Internet—and particularly how the students and teacher involved dealt with learning about it together.

As Wini Wood, who coordinates the Writing Program at Wellesley College in the United States, notes:

> *Along the way, we made some discoveries, stumbled on some problems, and worked our way through to some solutions. We—my students and I alike—consider these stumblings to be an important part of our learning experience.*

Another element of this Web-based project that we like is how new directions and outcomes for learning present themselves when Internet experiences become part of the classroom experience.

Thanks to Wini for describing how this happened in her Strong Women in Film *course.*

INTRODUCTION: TWO SMALL STORIES AND SOME QUESTIONS

When I first brought my writing class to the Web, it was because several students doing research about the contemporary Polish film *Blue* were having trouble finding information. "Why don't we search on the Web?" I suggested, and within seconds, we found four or five good sites about both the film and the director.

And we also found sound! With a click of the mouse, we filled the classroom with *Blue's* elegiac theme song (you can find it too, at: http://www.petey.com/kk/bluflute.mid). Meanwhile, in another corner of the room, a second group—those investigating Disney's *The Little Mermaid*—had surreptitiously followed our lead, and before we knew it, the calypso beat of "Under the Sea" was competing with the piano strains of "Blue." We all burst into helpless laughter.

The following semester, I introduced the Web as a research tool right away, using *Blue* as my demonstration example. "It won't do you any good to search for this particular film's title," I explained to the class officiously. "If you search for *Blue*, you'll turn up millions of different kinds of sites, probably none of them having to do with the movie. Let's search by the director's name, Krzysztof Kieslowski." I wrote the words on the board and returned to the demonstration computer to start my search. "He just died!" murmured one of the students, in disbelief, from behind her terminal. Her search—performed while I was writing on the board—had turned up an obituary. Kieslowski had died the day before, and we learned of it together, in class, before the news had reached the major newspapers. This time it was sadness, not laughter, that filled the classroom. (Kieslowski Tribute pages: http://cinemania.msn.com/cinemania/features/FeatureKieslowski.htm)

All this, and more, is the World Wide Web. It is a place where meaning is made and knowledge formed continually, often before your very eyes. It is a place where you can locate information before it appears in print sources. It is a place where students can upstage their teachers. It is a place of crazy juxtapositions, where word and picture and sound all come together to create meaning and memory. It is a place that prompts students to ask "Why?" and "What does this mean?" and, before very long, "Can I do this, too?"

Why, my students asked, is there a site called Ariel's Fan Club that seems to have only men as members? Why is Joan Crawford in *Mildred Pierce* an icon for gay men? Why are we as a class amused when we pull down a sound clip of Meg Ryan's comic heavy breathing in *When Harry Met Sally?* but offended by a site called "Altar to Meg Ryan"? Would other people react differently to these sites than we do, and why? What does this tell us about how people view film—and about the many ways images of women in film are open to interpretation? What is the usefulness of the various sites we have found: to provide information, to provide interesting criticism, to provide a window onto the viewing public? What is the range of our own responses, both to the films we view and the sites we browse? What makes us feel simple pleasure, what touches us, what offends us, what stimulates us to think, what moves us to action?

THE WEB IN OUR COURSE, OUR COURSE ON THE WEB

The topic of this particular class (a first-year writing course at Wellesley College) was women in film; the course emphasizes critical awareness, writing skills, and research skills. Students view, discuss, and write about six classic Hollywood films made between 1933 and 1994; for their final project, working in groups, they select, research, and write about a film of their choice (contemporary or not, Hollywood or not). During the semester I am describing here, we linked our work on the Web directly to the intellectual project of the course—a study of the representation of women in film. We used the Web in two ways: first, for research purposes, and second, for publication, collaborating to produce a Web page that provides a snapshot of our course (this site is available for your viewing pleasure at **http://www.wellesley.edu/Writing/Strongwomen/index.html**). Below are some of the exercises and activities we undertook in each part of the course.

A. Doing Research on Films

During the first half of the semester, the exercises are designed to compare Web-based research to print-based research; the assignments move from the simple (locating factual information) to the complex (assessing criticism, discovering different points of view). But all exercises, even the simplest, ask students to think and to question. Here are some of my favorite research exercises:

1. *The facts, ma'am, just the facts.* When they write about a movie, I want to be sure my students use the facts accurately—they should know the director, date of release, actors and characters' names of any movie they write about (and they should spell them correctly!). I hand out my own fact sheets for the first movies we view, but as the semester progresses, we take a trip to the library to learn about film reference books, and then students must produce their own fact sheets. In one exercise, I ask them to compare standard print reference sources (e.g., *Magills*) with standard Internet reference resources (the *Internet Movie Database* is my favorite: **http://www.imdb.com/**). What are the strengths and limitations of each?

2. *Group data blitz.* For every movie we study in class (e.g., *Casablanca*), everyone in the class searches for everything she can find about the movie on the Web. We work in groups, and one group searches by director's name, another by film title, another by the names of famous actors or actresses in the film. As we search, we pool our findings in a class electronic database (our writing lab is equipped with the Daedalus Integrated Writing System, and we copy and paste the URLs of the sites we find into DIWS's chat space, together with a brief description/review of the site.) We quickly learn that if we keep accurate and informative records of the sites we have visited, we have a good log that we can easily edit later on into either a bibliography or a page of links.

3. *Evaluation of the findings.* We then discuss the sites we've found. What is the nature of each site? Is it a personal, academic, or commercial site? What motivated the author to produce it? What kind of audience is the author trying to reach? What is the relative balance between information, graphics, and links? Is the site easy to navigate? Which sites do you like the best, and why? What makes a site a good one? And finally, when we think about all these sites together, what do they tell us about how different kinds of viewers see this film?

4. *Interact!* Websurfers can now practice using their writing and critical skills with a real audience by posting directly to some sites.

Mr. Cranky's Reviews (**http://internet-plaza.net/zone/mrcranky/**), for example, has a guestbook space where you can add your own comments. Or you can email the author of a page directly, or you can record your rating of a particular film at the *Internet Movie Database* (**http://www.imdb.com/**).

B. Planning and Producing a Web Site

This much surfing and scrutiny of Web sites makes a person itch to make her own site, and it wasn't long before our class decided that we wanted to make our presence felt on the Web. For one thing, we wanted to try our hands at doing what looked like so much fun—mingling sound and graphics with text, layering it into the pages that make up a site, posting information, commentary, and opinion for all the world to see. But more important, we had discovered, as a group, that we wanted to speak back to the Web. The class felt that many Web writers were not treating women in film with respect, and we wanted to create a site that foregrounded women's roles ethically and responsibly. The students also wanted to create a site that showed what they were learning in class—that provided information about the older movies they were discovering, and that provided a mirror of our class's activities. Our chief goal, as we designed and laid out the site, was to say what *we* thought about the representation of women in film.

We managed to plan and put together our own Web site with very little effort, working mostly outside of class time (because I hadn't really planned class time for this activity). Two volunteers from the class designed the site on paper; I translated it into HTML and brought a draft of the page to class for critique. Many of the links and words on the page were drawn from what different students had already written—in their research logs and their papers. It did not take long for us to cut and paste their words into a skeleton of the page. Along the way, we made some discoveries, stumbled on some problems, and came up with some solutions. We—my students and I alike—consider these stumblings to be an important part of our learning experience.

CRAFTING A COLLABORATIVE WEB PAGE: PROBLEMS AND SOLUTIONS

Problem One: How to Show Our Multiplicity of Voices?

This was a pleasant problem. As we tried to copy, paste, and weave together fragments of material that we had already written, we discovered that we had written in many kinds of voices—voices of pleasure, funk, wit, criticism, serious analysis. And these many voices came not just from different students, but often, from one person writing at different times. Should we rewrite everything to present a single unified voice? Or should we preserve the cacophony and multiplicity that we were discovering? We opted for the latter, and we like that choice, although it reduces the coherence of our site.

Problem Two: Not Everyone in the Class Held the Same View

This is the unpleasant side of problem one. It is one thing to deal with different voices; it is a different thing entirely to deal with opposing opinions! Some students felt, for example, that our site should be strongly feminist in nature; others argued that an overly feminist tone would turn away the very browsers we wanted most to speak to. Some students wanted funk; others wanted seriousness. Some wanted more text; others wanted more pictures. We have not fully resolved any of these debates (we never will), but having them has taught us a lot about collaboration, about rhetorical choices and the thinking that lies behind them, and about argument and decision-making. In the end, our Web site shows some of this conflict—different portions of the site demonstrate different opinions and approaches. We decided, again, to sacrifice perfect coherence for a display of our differences.

Problem Three: Some of the Sites We Wanted to Link to Presented Views That Differed from Ours

We found that we didn't want to avoid linking to these sites (unless they were really offensive, in which case we didn't want to support them in any way), but rather wanted to address the differences between their views and ours directly, usually with the text surrounding our links. In this way, we made our Web site into an argument—a site that "talks back" to the sites we link to. We are still not sure whether our "argument" is visible and tenable to those who visit our site.

Problem Four: Copyright Law

One day, in class, as we were checking a link to a site we admired, one filled with images from *Casablanca*, we discovered that all the images had disappeared! In their place was a sad note; the author of that site had been required, by the owner of the *Casablanca* copyright, to remove all his images from the Web. We were crushed and disappointed; not only did we miss this beautiful site, but we also realized that our own use of images would be more limited than we had imagined. But we had a good discussion about copyright law and plagiarism; we learned firsthand what was legal and what was not; we learned what we wanted to protest and what we were bound to accept. We discussed ways to request permission to use an image. (Note: An excellent source of links to information about intellectual property is this site, create by Jeff Galin: **http://www.pitt.edu/~hypertch/ copyright.html#header4**).

CONCLUSION: THE END IS NOT THE END

And so we ended the semester with a skeleton of a Web page and some interesting problems. But the story does not end there. A year later, the class continues to work on the Web site (it is vastly different now from what it was in May 1996), and I know that the next time I teach this course, my new class, starting with this Web site already in place, will come up with new ideas.

CHAPTER 26

Taming the Tube and NewsWave

by
Dalia M. Naujokaitis
Special Assignment Teacher
St. Elizabeth Catholic School
Ottawa, Ontario

Title	Taming the Tube and NewsWave
Level	Middle School, Secondary
Type	Focus on information; interaction; task
Tool(s)	Email, listserv, web
Contact	Dalia Naujokaitis dalia@sympatico.ca

Dalia Naujokaitis has created a number of innovative, Internet-based learning projects with her students at St. Elizabeth Catholic School in Ottawa. It may surprise you to learn that her pupils are elementary school students and that we have included their work here, given that most students reading this book are likely to be enrolled at secondary and post-secondary institutions. However, we have some very good reasons for doing so.

First, Dalia's projects involve students in a variety of grades, and provide useful demonstrations of the value of learning through projects, which is, after all, the focus of this section. We encourage you to consider the design of these projects, and how they might serve your own interests, particularly in classes that also meet face to face. A second reason is that, like some of the other projects profiled here, they demonstrate how the approaches to learning undertaken at one level establish skills that can be applied at another. And third, the transferable nature of these projects can be seen in how technologies are used, from email and listservs to multimedia and the World Wide Web.

"Since 1994, students in my class have been collaborating with other classes worldwide," writes Dalia, noting that these projects integrate subjects such as science, mathematics, creative problem-solving, and telecommunications. *"They are encouraged to explore new hypotheses, search out new sources of information and acquire the navigational tools of the information highway."*

But it hasn't always been easy, which is another thing we like about the perspective Dalia and her students have adopted as a result of their development of, and participation in, these projects.

"The process of creating, implementing and evaluating our collaborative, multidisciplinary learning projects on the Internet has sometimes been daunting," she remarks. "At the start we felt like explorers in uncharted waters without a compass. But we have persevered...."

In the end their perseverance paid off. Several of their projects have won national and international recognition, including a Prime Minister's Award for Teaching Excellence in Science, Technology, and Mathematics, and the Roy C. Hill Award for Innovation in Teaching, as well as honorable mentions in ISTE's Telecomputing Activity Plan contests in 1995 and 1996, respectively.

Our thanks to Dalia for telling us about these projects here.

MAKING THE WORLD OUR CLASSROOM: ADVENTURES IN PROJECT-BASED LEARNING ON THE INTERNET

To date I have created and implemented with my students eight Internet learning projects. Originally our projects relied heavily on email, but with access to the World Wide Web each has become an interactive Web site, and some projects have included other new technologies such as videoconferencing and multimedia. Funding for the hardware and software needed has come from my school board, from the GrassRoots Projects program of Canada's SchoolNet, and from several awards.

Taming the Tube, a student-run survey and analysis (via the Internet) of the TV-watching

Project 1:	Taming the Tube: TV-Watching Habits of ten- to twelve-year-olds
Website:	http://www3.sympatico.ca/dalia/tametube/intro.htm
Level:	Grades four to seven (ages ten to twelve)
Tools:	Email, WWW, listserver
Timeline:	January to April, annually since 1994
Contact:	Dalia Naujokaitis St. Elizabeth School, Ottawa, Ontario
Email:	dalia@sympatico.ca

habits of ten- to twelve-year-olds around the world, has attracted some three thousand participants annually since 1994, from close to three hundred classrooms in seven countries on four continents. Mounted on its own listserver on Canada's SchoolNet, the project provides a forum for junior-level students to do research using information technology. Students become scientists conducting research on an activity in which they have all participated: TV-watching. The participants collect answers to the following questions:

- How much TV is watched per week by ten- to twelve-year-olds?
- Who watches more TV, the girls or the boys?
- Are there any geographical differences?
- What are the favorite TV shows of people in this age group?

- How does TV influence the attitudes and lifestyles of ten- to twelve-year-olds?

Student researchers between the ages of ten and twelve from around the world gather and organize data in three activities. First, they record their own daily TV-watching times over the course of a week, and analyze their data by determining the mean, mode, median, and range of the findings for girls, boys, and the combined class. Second, they note their favorite TV shows, and any gender differences in what is watched. Third, the participants fill out a supplementary attitudes and lifestyles questionnaire devised by the St. Elizabeth's students, which looks at such topics as violence, role models, and advertising on TV. All the numeric and anecdotal data is returned to the Ottawa Tube Tamers so that they can record it and analyze it, using spreadsheets and databases, to do so. Prior to the data's arrival they were asked to devise hypotheses, and they now test them against the real-world data obtained, and seek explanations for divergences. Statistical data of individual classes and global results are shared with all participants via the listserver and the Web site.

Curriculum cross-fertilization and even extracurricular activities result from the interaction between classes on the Internet. For example, an Ontario grade eleven teacher incorporated *Taming the Tube* into his course Society: Challenge and Change as an independent study component: his high-school students went into elementary schools to run the project there with the target age group. In British Columbia and in Virginia and Washington, where parents were involved in the research, concern about the results of the survey led to parent-school committees being formed to provide alternative activities to watching TV after school.

Taming the Tube has been instrumental in getting students from diverse cultures to work cooperatively on a common goal. The project has generated enthusiasm for science, technology, and mathematics not only among the gifted students coordinating the project, but in the many mainstream classes participating. Locating fellow researchers worldwide using the principles of latitude and longitude meant geography skills were practiced in a real-life context. The exchange of "hello" letters among the participants encouraged cross-cultural dialogue, tolerance for and understanding of diverse perspectives.

All the participants were doing real science and mathematics in a collaborative setting involving real-world interaction. As they did so, they acquired hands-on skills. They applied the scientific method in a concrete and useful way and shared their findings with a real audience. The students became proficient with telecommunications and acquired skills both in data management and analysis by using computer technology.

Project 2:	NewsWave Canada
Website:	http://home.on.rogers.wave.ca/eliza/newswave/
Level:	Grades three to eleven (ages eight to sixteen)
Tools:	Email, WWW, listserver
Timeline:	Published online four times a year
Contact:	Dalia Naujokaitis St. Elizabeth School, Ottawa, Ontario
Email:	dalia@sympatico.ca

NewsWave Canada, the first Canadian online news magazine created, illustrated, and published by students for students aged eight to sixteen was launched on the Web in the fall of 1995 to celebrate the fiftieth anniversary of the United Nations. This interdisciplinary Internet learning project serves as a forum for students from grades three to twelve writing from across Canada and the world. It enables them to learn about issues of local, national, and global importance through online dialogue. NewsWave is published four times a year and each issue has a theme that is easily integrated into the curriculum. There are many issues currently available online. Ongoing features also provide a great place for students to publish their writings.

HOW DID THIS ELECTRONIC PUBLISHING PHENOMENON HAPPEN?
With great anticipation in the fall of 1995 a call to participate in NewsWave Canada was posted by the grade six PGL and regular class students at St. Elizabeth's on Canada's SchoolNet listserver.

And then we waited…wondering whether our efforts would pay off or whether our brainchild would be lost somewhere in cyberspace. We wanted to create an online student news magazine that would reflect the diversity of Canada and allow students of all ages to communicate and publish on contemporary, real-world topics and have fun at the same time. While we waited we wondered, Will anyone be interested enough to join? Was all that planning for naught? How many schools will register? But we need not have worried. NewsWave Canada had an easy birth.

For the inaugural issue, forty classes truly reflective of Canada's diversity, participated from coast to coast. We were all there together: Yukon, the Northwest Territories, British Columbia, Alberta, Manitoba, Saskatchewan, Ontario, Quebec, Newfoundland, Nova Scotia, and New Brunswick, the isolated hamlets, the big cities, the suburbs, the logging towns and the fishing villages.…

HOW DOES NEWSWAVE ACTUALLY WORK?
Participating students from across the country write news articles and upload them on the NewsWave listserver, provided for us by Canada's SchoolNet, to create their own electronic "wire service." Each participating class then chooses what materials to download in order to publish its own print newspaper or newsletter. Meanwhile, the students at St. Elizabeth School in Ottawa (nicknamed "The pugglers") use the uploaded articles to create, manage, and publish NewsWave Canada elec-

tronically on the World Wide Web for the whole world to see.

Students who participate in this multidimensional project not only become researchers and analysts but also writers and publishers. They develop skills needed in the information age. Through the use of technology they gather, analyze, process, and communicate information dealing with contemporary issues in the real world.

AND WE HAVEN'T LOOKED BACK...

As of June 1997 more than two hundred classes worldwide have participated in NewsWave. We are now an official SchoolNet GrassRoots project sponsored by Rogerswave, which provides us with free space on its server. We have learned all about HTML, CorelDraw, FTP, and the World Wide Web. We have met students all over the world via the Internet; and, in addition to the awards noted in the Introduction, we have received "Cool Site" designations and won children's literature online contests. Not bad for a bunch of eleven-year-olds, eh?

CYBEREVENTS

Not all Web sites are created equal. The sites we enjoyed were those that were updated often, were interactive and provided opportunities for feedback and collaboration. NewsWave was flourishing and succeeded in providing lots of reading material, but something was needed to jazz it up and make it inviting and challenging all year long. Online activities that were ongoing or seasonal could do this and would not be too taxing technically for participants. So we coined a new word, "CyberEvent," and we started designing interactive mini-projects for NewsWave.

Some of them soon took on a life of their own. Spawned by NewsWave, they could be accessed separately via the magic of Internet links. There are several of these CyberEvents. One, *Cyberstumpers* (**http://home.on.rogers.wave.ca/ eliza/newswave/fun/jffun.htm**), is the "just for fun" section of NewsWave. It contains riddles, jokes, and problems that are guaranteed to make you think! Contributions from readers are welcome.

Another CyberEvent, *The Gallery of Unsung Heroes and Heroines* (**http://home.on.rogers.wave.ca/ eliza/cyber/front.htm**), was created by the PGL class of 1996–97 with the help of students (ages eight to sixteen) from eighteen schools around the world. The Gallery celebrates and honors ordinary people who have made a difference in other people's lives. Through online dialogue students brainstorm and debate the qualities of heroism. Then they interview and profile their local heroes and heroines. The profiles they gather are used by the students at St. Elizabeth to create The Gallery on the Web.

This site not only provides an international cyberplace where students may nominate other heroes, but it also serves as a resource for the global community for insights into the qualities of persons who inspire and provide role models for youth. In the spring of 1997, it placed second in the category of Community and Special Populations in the International Schools Cyberfair '97 (Global SchoolNet Foundation), in which more than 350 schools participated worldwide. The Gallery also won second place in the A&E Television Network Teacher Grant competition, which was open to all schools across Canada, and was a winning entry in

ISTE's *Telecomputing Activity Plan* contest (1997).

In *Learning: The Next Generation* (**http://home.on.rogers.wave.ca/eliza/learn/ front.htm**) students investigate the impact of technology on teaching and learning. As architects they design schools of the future and share their blueprints via videoconferencing with participating schools. As journalists they research what life will be like in the next millennium and report their findings in "Shocked," a news magazine dedicated to all things wired and futuristic.

The inaugural version of this ongoing CyberEvent was the basis for an experimental cross-border collaboration between St. Elizabeth's in Ottawa and Burrville Elementary School in Washington, D.C., under the aegis of Canada's SchoolNet. It was showcased as part of the Chretien state visit to Washington in April 1997.

LESSONS LEARNED, DISCOVERIES MADE

As we became more adept and confident in designing and running online projects, we realized that planning is essential to a project's success. The other insights we gained can be categorized under three general headings.

LESSON ONE: Organizational Requirements or The Nitty Gritty of Project-based Learning on the Internet

The success of any online learning project lies in following a few basic guidelines:

Get hooked on curriculum. Design your project with specific curriculum outcomes in mind both for students and for teachers. Online activities are not add-ons or something one does in the classroom when one has time. They are another way of teaching and learning. If your goals are not closely aligned with curriculum objectives, there may not be many takers when you advertise your project.

Detail the details. Advertise your Call to Participate on several educational listservers, at least six to eight weeks before the project is to start. Be very specific in outlining procedures, timelines, and deadlines in the project. You may have a very clear idea of where you are heading, but your participants will need reminders just in case that sheet with all the information vanishes from the bulletin board or gets lost when the computer system crashes.

Collaborate, don't isolate. Make sure that your project encourages dialogue, cooperative planning and evaluation, sharing of resources and ideas. Provide lots of electronic feedback and encouragement to participants. Cyberspace can be a very intimidating place, especially for newcomers. Train your students to be cyber-ambassadors through email. Everyone loves receiving mail!

Validate, don't regurgitate. Searching the Internet for information can be a daunting task. When the information is found, unless your source is well known, you have no proof that the information is correct or current. Be critical, check out your sources, and validate your findings. And learn how to reference Internet sources correctly. Just because this information is free, doesn't mean you can present it as your own work. Plagiarism is still plagiarism no matter how you cut it.

Expect the unexpected. Technology is great when it works. Be patient if it sometimes has a mind of its own. Give yourself more time and more scope to finish a task. If you need the technology right away, that is when it just might fail you.... (Murphy's Law)

Have a chuckle. Retain your sense of humor.... It will come in handy especially when HTML gets a mind of its own or the server is down and you needed it yesterday.

LESSON TWO: Tools and Skills for the Next Generation or How to Keep Smiling through a Killer Learning Curve

While designing online projects presented a challenge, we found that implementing the same project demanded that a certain subset of skills be in place or be acquired *very quickly* both by teachers and students. These skills fall into two main areas: technical/computer skills and cooperative learning strategies. We found that these skills were essential to the smooth running and enjoyment of online activity. Training and technical support in these two areas throughout the project are essential for success.

Technical/Computer Skills. Without a doubt touching the computer does not transform the toucher, but a comfort level in using the computer is essential for the project to run smoothly. This part of the project is always the most daunting. There is so much to learn, in so little time, with so few computers and technology is constantly changing. Both students and teachers need to acquire basic Internet skills. They must know how to send email, how to connect to the network, how to navigate the World Wide Web, and how to use search engines. Since all our projects became Web sites, software and techniques for illustrating, creating, and managing the home pages had to be learned (e.g., HTML, CorelDraw, LV-Pro and GIF Construction Kit and image digitization).

Cooperative Learning. The success of online projects depends on the cooperation and teamwork of the participants. This teamwork needs to happen especially in the class that is running the project. Just putting students into teams does *not* ensure cooperative problem-solving and decision-making. Both students and teachers must learn how to apply cooperative strategies to group learning. Whether one follows the Johnson and Johnson or the Kagan cooperative learning model, using a definite strategy facilitates effective small group learning and problem-solving.

Monitoring the Learning Curve. I devised an effective Skill Assessment Survey to evaluate both teachers' and students' computer skills. And of course, as predicted, everyone's level of knowledge varied and there was so much to learn!

Together with the students, I created a training plan that took into account the rapid rate at which technology changes and evolves. I trained my core group of students. If I was unfamiliar with a concept, I assigned a student or a team of students to investigate and report back to the group. We formed cooperative teams and assigned one student mentor to each team. And so the training of the troops began not in isolation but as part of the project.

I found that my students approached training with the same enthusiasm as achieving an advanced level of a Nintendo game. They were absolutely fearless and very willing to share their expertise with the less confident adults and classmates. We learned together through practice, more training and more practice. Learning is never finished, something new always lies around the next corner....

LESSON THREE: The Web as a Transformational Technology or Shifting Gears to New Paradigms for Teaching and Learning

The most exciting lesson of our online adventures has been the realization that we have at our fingertips a technology that is transforming both learning and teaching, namely the World Wide Web. Business is "not as usual" in our classrooms as we begin to create electronic, networked learning communities.

I see the World Wide Web not as a passive tool that delivers information or a glorified electronic "show-and-tell" bulletin board where students can display their work but rather as a dynamic and interactive medium that promotes a different way of teaching and learning. It encourages participation, resource building, and above all communication and the sharing of ideas.

I believe that our students must not only learn to use technology, but must also acquire sound communication skills, flexibility, resourcefulness, problem-solving techniques, and the ability to work as members of a team. That's what I've been trying to give them in my classroom and in collaboration with other teachers across the Internet.

Through the Web, students become the creators and not only the consumers of knowledge. Project-based online learning blends traditional subject-driven goals with the objectives of authentic real-world education. We found that our projects that dealt with real issues, whether the TV-watching habits of ten- to twelve-year-olds or the impact of technology on teaching and learning, provided excellent opportunities for students to locate information, design experiments, test hypotheses, solve problems online, and communicate with other students across Canada and the globe. The students were highly motivated and delighted in publishing their findings to a real audience on the Web.

And I am the luckiest teacher I know, as my job allows me to explore new technologies along with the students. My role has changed dramatically, as I am now more an observer, a co-learner, and a facilitator in a class where cooperative learning, inquiry, online collaboration and investigation are regular fare. The wave of the future is here: teamwork, telecommunications, and transformation. Will we be ready for the next shifting of gears?

CHAPTER 27

Writing in the Matrix: Tapping the Living Database of Experts on the Internet

by
Dr. Michael J. Day
Associate Professor of English
Department of Humanities
South Dakota School of Mines and Technology
Rapid City, South Dakota

Title	Writing in the Matrix: Tapping the Living Database of Experts on the Internet
Level	Post Secondary
Type	Focus on interaction; task
Tool(s)	Email, listserv, Web
Contact	Michael J. Day mday@silver.sdsmt.edu http://silver.sdsmt.edu/~mday

Are you considering a technical or professional program at the post-secondary level? If so, then Writing in the Matrix *is an example of how the Internet can be used to involve yourself in the professional or technical writing of the field you are considering.*

PROFESSIONAL DISCUSSION

In our experience involvement in professional discussion is a major use of online communication. In education, for instance, many teachers seek opportunities to discuss their profession. In a way it is a kind of professional development process that people can participate in when it is useful to do so and when they have time available, or need to involve themselves.

Professional discussion often occurs when one's involvement in an activity of interest causes participants to engage one another in ways that draw on their professional or technical interests. You can bet, for example, that the writers and teachers participating in the Writers in Electronic Residence program like to interact with other writers and teachers in addition to students online. If you take a look at any of the Internet projects profiled in this book, you can imagine how participants might engage one another.

WRITING TO LEARN

Your experiences with others on the Internet are likely to encourage you and lead you to see things in new ways. Indeed, your own learning will come partly from these experiences. But it will also come partly from the discussions you have about your experiences. We have already noted how this happens in the classroom, particularly at the secondary level, where classes meet regularly and can participate in group activities fairly easily.

This process has a lot to do with the ways in which we use language. We are all familiar with using language to communicate our ideas to others verbally, in print, and sometimes in sign. This can be described as using language to be understood. However, we also use language to be communicated to, and to make what we receive meaningful. Learning in this way can be described as using language to understand.

As Michael's project demonstrates, this kind of discussion can also happen online, and we encourage you to participate in it, just as he has in his role as chair of the National Council of Teachers of English (NCTE) Assembly of Computers in English, and as co-director of the Great Plains Alliance for Computers and Writing.

We'd like to thank Michael for updating us about his work in this edition of The Learning Highway.

OVERVIEW

Students in most writing classes produce papers for which the primary audience is the teacher and the primary purpose is to pass the course. Yet our study of rhetoric tells us that citizens need to be prepared to write for a variety of audiences in a variety of contexts. With the proliferation of the Internet, more and more students have access to what Howard Rheingold calls a "living database" of people grouped into virtual communities with similar interests. By first monitoring discussion groups on the network to analyze the audience and discourse conventions used there, then posting messages to these groups, students can gain experience writing for real audiences spanning the globe. At the same time, they can gather the type of information for research projects that only human respondents can provide.

ACTIVITY AND PURPOSE

After being brought up to speed on the local electronic mail system, students select networked discussion groups of interest to them from sources such as the List of Lists (**http://www.liszt.com/**). These groups may include those distributed by listserv and those on Usenet and local bulletin board systems. Students then monitor discussion for about two weeks, discuss rhetorical strategies and audience in class, and write a short report on the topic and discourse conventions they find. Finally, they post one to five messages to the group or to selected members.

The goal is to allow them to familiarize themselves with the discourse conventions and topics of their chosen fields or interests, so that they might practice using those conventions, discussing those topics, and making connections with other students and professionals in those fields or with those interests. They thus become situated in the discourse community of their profession or interest, and come to understand how such communities are built and maintained. Further, they get practice with a rather new form of information gathering made possible when geographically separate but like-minded people work together to answer questions and solve problems.

MATERIALS/FACILITIES

Each student needs an Internet account and access to a connected computer. A class with only one or two accounts might be able to do an abbreviated version of this activity by sharing the account among several students. Students will also usually require some training in basic email, netiquette, and manipulating files.

CURRENT CONTEXT

English 379 is an upper-level required class in advanced technical communications at a state technical university. The goal of the course is to teach primarily engineering and science students how to communicate effectively on the job and in a variety of institutional settings. In addition to oral presentation and memo-, report-, proposal-, and manual-writing skills, the students are now encouraged to learn and use computer-mediated communication for collaboration and information exchange. This new direction takes into consideration the veritable paradigm shift we have seen in business and research communications toward greater and greater use of email, email discussion groups, real-time conferencing, and so on. The students in this class usually join technical discussion groups, but some also join hobby and social groups. As outlined above, writing classes such as high school or freshman year composition can also make productive use of such an activity.

PROCEDURE

1. Have all students in the class get email accounts, if possible.

2. Train them, or have your computer specialists train them, in basic email, Internet functions, and manipulating files.

3. Show them how to get access to the List of Lists and other databases of networked discussion groups, and ask them to choose one or two groups.

4. Show them how to subscribe, and have them help each other subscribe. Assign them to monitor the group's activity to gather information for a report on topics and conventions.

5. After the reports are turned in and the various conventions are discussed by the class, give them the assignment to send one to five messages to the group or to the individual.

The message can be:

A. an answer to someone's query;

B. a question related to a project the student is working on;

C. a general observation or comment on an event or issue.

The subprocess:

A. Compose a draft of the message and email it to a classmate who acts as peer critic for aspects of mechanics and style.

B. Upon receipt of the critique, revise and send the message to the group or individual.

C. Save all messages that provide the context for the posting, including the peer critique and the messages from the group or individual.

D. Send these messages by email as a sort of portfolio to the instructor for evaluation. Alternatively, print them out and hand them in.

FURTHER NOTES

1. Ethos

The discussion-group activity provides an ideal focus for class discussions of the rhetorical concept of ethos, the ability to build character, credibility, and authority with an audience through words. Students come to understand that if the group is to accept and answer their contributions, they need to use rhetorical strategies that give them the persona of a concerned and professional writer. They often do not get responses if they take on the "Gee, I'm just a poor inexperienced student doing a class assignment" attitude. They learn to use language to achieve a desired effect for a particular audience.

2. Research Projects

I encourage my students to join groups related to the topic of their final research projects, and to use the groups as sounding boards for some of the questions they need to answer. They have had success administering questionnaires to group members, getting opinions from experts, and having books and articles recommended to them. The information they gather then becomes part of a final research project, which is often a proposal or technical report. And because of the give-and-take of these discussion groups, they often find themselves in the position of the expert, gaining confidence from being able to make recommendations to others.

3. Evaluation

Evaluation is always a thorny issue, since adding the grading hand of the teacher to the equation shifts the audience back to the teacher. Many writing instructors who use electronic mail have suggested that it is best to leave assignments of this sort ungraded so that students can gain confidence in their abilities and know that they are truly writing to an outside audience. Peer critiques and self-evaluations may be a compromise, and some instructors have reported success with this activity despite having to put a grade on electronic mail messages.

UPDATE 1997

In 1995, members of my class developed a variation on the assignment. Students in one group decided that since they needed additional information about an article, they would email the author with questions. Never mind that the author was the well-known artificial intelligence pioneer Dr. Marvin Minsky of MIT; they were confident that if they wrote an effective message Dr. Minsky would respond. I doubted that we would get a response but was amazed when Dr. Minsky not only responded but gave detailed answers to my students.

Another group had similar success emailing a pioneer in HIV research at Berkeley. As with the postings to professional discussion groups, the students' ability to write clear, persuasive, and professional-sounding inquiries was instrumental in receiving responses from the experts.

My classes now all have their own email discussion groups in which the students discuss course issues, work on their assignments, and give each other advice. I have found that in writing classes such discussion groups provide students with a forum for a different kind of writing that is more conversational and that builds a sense of a class community. I do not grade their contributions, but I do require that students participate to a certain degree so that none of them will miss out on the experience.

The latest network technology allows all of our class discussion to be archived at a World Wide Web site, which is linked to our class Web page. Our conversations are then easily accessible even if students lose email messages. If the class wants privacy, the messages can be archived at an address only the students know; if they wish to make their conversations public, the archive can be linked to publicly accessible sites.

CHAPTER 28

Writers in Electronic Residence

by
Trevor Owen
Program Director, Writers in Electronic
    Residence
Faculty of Education, York University

Title	Writers in Electronic Residence
Level	K–12, Post Secondary, Teacher Education
Type	Focus on interaction; task
Tool(s)	Computer-conferencing, Web
Contact	Trevor Owen wier@edu.yorku.ca http://www.wier.yorku.ca/WIERhome/

Writers in Electronic Residence (WIER) links Canada's writers with Canada's schools in an exchange of original writing and commentary. Well-known authors join classrooms electronically to read and discuss the students' creative writing. Classes also receive books by the authors with whom they are working online.

In addition to its conferencing-based creative writing programs, WIER offers information at its Web site, including authors' biographies, student writing samples, and resources for writing and educators. It also has other pages, like "Cool Poem of the Week," which features student writing from WIER, and "Canadian Author of the Month," which features biographies of the online authors.

WIER is a national program, offering twelve-week programs at each of the elementary, middle school, and secondary levels each fall, winter, and spring. We looked at WIER in Chapter 3 when we were considering how learning on the Internet applies to everyone—students and teachers. This chapter, which will interest students of creative writing, as well as student teachers, takes a closer look at the program, and how it has developed since it began in 1988.

THE STORY OF WIER

The idea for WIER came in 1984. I had heard about *SwiftCurrent*, an "electronic literary magazine," which invited established authors to serve as "contributing editors" and provided them with access to one another in a national professional dialogue. In keeping with the metaphor of magazine publishing, *SwiftCurrent*'s online "subscribers" were invited to purchase subscriptions, which provided read-only access to recent works by the authors. Subscribers could tailor the contents of *SwiftCurrent* by deleting the entries they didn't want to read.

I thought *SwiftCurrent* was a great idea, and that a similar initiative linking writers with students would make a useful contribution both to teaching and learning in the classroom, as well as to the use of technology to support creative writing, and to the appreciation of Canadian literature. However, although the organizers of *SwiftCurrent* supported the idea, they saw it as beyond their scope. They did permit a few email-based exchanges between writers on their system and the students in my class, but I was ultimately not successful in getting WIER off the ground until 1988. At that time, I proposed undertaking a simple email-based project between one writer and my class, and a number of the *SwiftCurrent* authors expressed interest. One of these, Vancouver-based poet Lionel Kearns, took an active interest in the idea, and introduced me to Gerri Sinclair at the Faculty of Education at Simon Fraser University (SFU), in Vancouver, B.C. Thanks to their efforts, SFU offered to mount the project on its computer systems, and Lionel served as the first writer in electronic residence.

In 1989, WIER expanded to two writers and involved students from three schools. In the spring, novelist Katherine Govier became interested in the project, and joined in for the remainder of the year. Govier, who is well known for her involvement in Canada's writing community, participated in WIER for several years. As chair of the Writers' Development Trust (WDT), a national organization dedicated to advancing the cause of Canadian writers and writing, she saw an opportunity to promote WIER's growth through the Trust and, in the process, to generate more work opportunities for writers. In 1990, she guided the WDT to help administer WIER and to provide financial support through fund-raising.

In the spring of 1992, the Faculty of Education at York University assumed responsibility for pedagogical development and technological support for WIER from SFU in order to inform and advance online learning through teacher education and research. York opened its first WIER writing conference in January 1993. This came about thanks to the faculty's dean, Dr. Stan Shapson.

Today, WIER is administered by the Trust in partnership with York's Faculty of Education, working with corporate and government sponsors throughout Canada. WIER operates on a FirstClass conferencing system, which offers both a graphical-user interface (GUI) and a command line user interface (CLUI), located at York. The program is accessible over the Internet.

WHAT IS WIER?
WIER is a national program that operates in Canadian schools from coast to coast to coast. It involves thousands of students, hundreds of teachers, and a fine and growing coterie of writers who are interested in the new form of work that WIER creates—a feature of WIER that continues to develop in the writing com-

munity. As mentioned previously, there are programs for elementary (grades one to six), middle school (grades seven to nine) and secondary school students (grades nine to twelve), along with some post-secondary involvement in the community college system, and in university-based teacher education programs, in which student teachers undertake "virtual practicum" placements online. Writers and teachers who have experience with WIER serve as online moderators in each conference.

Although the program provides a clear example of the impact of technology on classroom life, WIER's primary purpose from the outset has had little to do with the technology that sustains it. Rather, WIER has always been rooted in linking students and their teachers with Canada's authors in an exchange of creative writing and related commentary.

How It Works

Students work offline before posting their work online; in fact, most of the students encounter WIER in print, reading the works of others in binders located in the classroom or library. They use word processors to compose their works and responses to the works of others before sending their writing to WIER's online conferences.

Most of the writing is poetry and short fiction. WIER encourages students to submit pieces they consider to be in draft stages—"writing they care enough about to want to work on more," as WIER author Kathy Stinson put it— rather than finished works in order to get the most from their interactions with writers and others on the system. Another reason for this is that the online discussions encourage writing in other forms, in response to particular issues or concerns expressed in one or more of the submissions. Not surprisingly, textual discussions develop online in which students explore their ideas with one another.

"Local Shape"

These discussions are normally supported as part of the activity associated with WIER in each of the participating classrooms, as students and teachers develop their understanding of online experiences in their own classrooms. WIER regards this mediation as central to the program's success, bringing a "local shape" to the online experience. The idea—that online learning happens partly online, but mostly in the classroom—frames an understanding of the electronic residency as a *community of interaction* that involves participants in the life of the classroom *and* the online conferences.

The Electronic Literary Salon

As mentioned previously, WIER operates a trimester model for all grades, offering programs in the fall, winter, and spring terms. Each term is twelve weeks long. This approach aligns the program with the range of semestered and term-based school calendars in Canada, and allows classes to participate in a timeframe that best suits their needs.

Classes are grouped in "electronic literary salons," normally comprising six classes from across the country. In turn, salons are grouped with one or two other salons to form a conference. WIER employs one professional Canadian writer for every six classes that participate in the program. All writers in a given conference work with all salons in that conference. This method of grouping salons and writers maintains the multiplicity of writers' voices that has become an integral part of the WIER experience. Each conference also has a teacher/moderator to help facilitate discussions.

PROGRAM STRUCTURE
Middle and Secondary Schools
Each term at the middle and secondary levels is structured as follows:

- two weeks: training, orientation, and introductions

- three weeks: new work and responses

- two weeks: student response period

- three weeks: new work and responses

- two weeks: student response period and closing activities

Elementary Schools
Younger children need longer intervals to prepare writing, so WIER's elementary level program is structured differently:

- two weeks: training, orientation, and introductions

- eight weeks: new work, responses, and interaction

- two weeks: closing activities

A PEDAGOGY OF TECHNOLOGY
WIER's understanding of educational telecommunications in general, and computer conferencing in particular, is that they are textual media capable of promoting *considered response* through written expression and interaction, building a reflective community, both online and in the classroom. WIER has come to understand that *online learning experiences are essentially experiences of language and task through interaction and reflection* more than they are *experiences of technology through access to information and the immediacy of its delivery*.

This understanding frames a pedagogy of technology that emphasizes change over production and guides WIER's operation. It is a pedagogy that emphasizes the use of technology as a *catalyst for learning* more than the use of technology as a "tool" of production.

A Reflective Community
It is this sense of seeing technology as a catalyst for learning that will be of greatest interest to students (and teachers and writers) who want to use new technologies as a means to inform and advance the work they do with one another. The communities they construct are written and considered. They are reflective communities that summon language—in written form online and in the classroom, and orally in the classroom—in contexts that are based on common interests in writing.

Certainly, this is a desired community for teachers involved in WIER. Throughout Canada, they report how they have "changed their teaching" in response to the manner in which the professional writers interact with the students in general, and how the writers focus on the writing more than on the student in particular. The most common expression of this change is how teachers alter their teaching and evaluation practices in order to spend more time responding to student writing *with* the students and less time "giving marks" or "marking kids" in isolation.

The result? One might expect reports from students, teachers, writers, and, in some cases, parents, to address how writing "improves," but more important than this are the reports of how students demonstrate a "greater investment" in their own learning as a result of having participated in a community of writing.

There are many examples of how the program has fostered writing and revision, as well as written interaction online and face-to-face interaction in the classroom, and I invite you to visit WIER's Web site to consider them.

WHAT HAPPENS NEXT?

The writers and students discuss each student's work, writer to writer. The responses and interactions are often lively and reveal less of a concern for an "evaluation" of the "quality" of writing in favor of conveying specific ideas about the work itself and the direction a student might consider for his or her own work, or might consider offering to another.

I can report, from personal observation in classrooms across Canada, as well as from the observations of numerous teachers and students over the years, that these responses from writers and others online in WIER have an impact in the classroom. Readers can easily imagine, I'm sure, what it must be like to be in school and receive a response to your work from a writer—especially from a writer whose book you may be reading at the time. There is a clear need to interpret the experience in the context of the local classroom, as students review the comments, and decide what they want to do with them. This is that sense of "local shape" I referred to previously.

The student writers may revise their works in response to the comments they receive. It may be that they will comment on the responses themselves and engage in a discussion about their work with others. Or they may decide to retain the version they originally posted online. In any case, the students will know more about the decisions they are capable of making as writers, and, more important, perhaps, *that* they can make them.

WIER encourages students to bring a sense of closure to the online discussions of their work as a way of demonstrating the value of acting on their decisions; however, it may be that the impact is felt more in classroom discussions than online and that a student may simply "move on" to other things without returning to the online forum.

FURTHER READING

Davey, F., and Wah, F. (1986). *The SwiftCurrent Anthology*. Toronto: Coach House Press.

Harasim, L. (1995). *Learning Networks*. Boston: MIT Press.

Mason, R. (1992). *Computer Conferencing: The Last Word*. Victoria: Beach Holme.

Owen, T. (1989). "Computer-mediated Writing and the Writer in Electronic Residence." In R. Mason & A. Kaye, eds., *Mindweave: Communication, Computers, and Distance Education* (pp. 208–211). Oxford, U.K.: Pergamon Press.

_____. (1990). "Waiting to Connect: The Writer in Electronic Residence." *The Computing Teacher*, 17(5): 46–49.

_____. (1991). "Online Learning Links Are

Language-Learning Links." *Output*, 12(1).

_____. (1995). "Poems That Change the World: Canada's Wired Writers," in *English Journal* 84(6).

_____. (1996). "An Odd Pleasure." In *The Nearness of You*, C. Edgar and S. Wood, eds. New York: Teachers and Writers Collaborative, pp. 151–67.

What Students Say

When we began working on this book, we invited people to become involved. The projects we have described came to us directly from the people who operate and participate in them, and we hope these examples have provided you with ideas and approaches that will help you use the Internet to act on your own intentions to learn.

We also heard from students who were not participating in any of these projects—students who just wanted to write and tell us about their experiences as Internet learners. In closing, then, we turn to the thoughts that a few of them sent along, as well as the reflections of one student who participated in one of the projects we describe.

The first two examples are drawn from both the secondary and post-secondary levels, and they reveal a good deal about what you may expect as you become an Internet learner. The next two pieces, from students studying at the graduate level, are also included for two reasons. First, because most of you will continue to learn on the Internet, we want to underscore the value of using what you have learned at one level and applying it at another. Second, their

focus on research and how Internet skills become general skills beyond school, will be helpful to many of you—no matter what level you are studying at just now.

Monica

Our first piece comes from Monica Downs, who wrote to us as a high-school freshman attending Hillsboro High School, in Hillsboro, North Dakota.

> I was first involved with Internet through a teacher who introduced me to a BBS system for students and teachers here. It was not, and has never been, an assigned project. This was the first time I had ever interacted with modems or anything similar. Once I had experimented and became familiar with it, I was hooked.
>
> The Internet has brought an entirely different view of the world into my own home. I now have the ability to have conversations with people from around the country, people from around the globe, daily.
>
> Last spring I was exchanging email with a group of high school students living in Israel.

They were studying the English language and one of their assignments was to discuss important topics with teenagers overseas. They asked me how I would feel if Jewish students were allowed to attend my high school. Evidently they attended a Muslim school that was considering allowing Jewish students to attend. They were very concerned about this, unsure of what people of this religion were really like. This blew me away. I knew that this part of the world was in conflict and that the two groups were segregated, but it had never hit me in the face like that before. I think that in America, younger people especially don't always realize how tolerant and accepting we are here. This experience really opened me up and showed me first hand what you read about in the newspapers every day.

Not only has Internet opened me up to different cultures from around the world and the U.S. alike, it has let me experience different opinions and express some of my own, freely. Forums, chat modes, and electronic student newspapers allow these things to happen. Many times debates are started over issues like politics, the environment, world peace, bigotry. All of a sudden students that never think twice about these things have a strong opinion and are actually willing to do independent research to prove their points. I've seen it first hand. Students who have never cared before develop causes. It is truly amazing. This also teaches kids that while it's definitely good to have your own opinions, it's equally important that others are able to express their opinions and that you are able to accept those opinions whether

you agree with them or not.

I definitely think that Internet should be introduced and available to students in the school systems. I do not believe, however, that it should be pushed at them by assigning projects based around it. Yes, it is a great learning tool, but I have a strong belief in individualism. Some kids are just not into computers like other kids are.

Internet is a wonderful experience. While I don't believe it should be a mandatory part of education, it should definitely be a strong option.

REFLECTIONS
We asked Monica to tell us whether she had found ways to incorporate Internet learning into her program at school. It turned out that she has...in a way....

"I've never used it to directly influence my curriculum other than my foreign language studies," Monica wrote back. "I take German classes and found a German student who is studying English. We converse over the Internet frequently in both languages. I think that this has made the learning of the language easier. The native German language is a little different from the book language, so this has taught me some of the slang."

We think it is interesting that no formal link was established between her learning and her courses for school. We also think it is worth noting that this doesn't matter much to Monica: "Internet is not part of the school's curriculum. It was introduced to me as an extra. I'm a person who enjoys learning and decided that it would be beneficial to me if I got more involved with Internet. I'm definitely glad I did get involved. It has been and will continue to be, I hope, a rewarding experience."

Marcia

Our next comment comes from Marcia Quinn, who wrote to us about her studies at Trent University in Peterborough, Ontario.

> I had an amazing experience with the Internet. I was researching an essay for my anthropology course, and having a lot of problems because the library here is very limited. I joined up with the sci.archaeology newsgroup and within 24 hours of sending my posting "for HELP," I received tons of information from people across the world who actually worked at the dig I had to write my paper on—Sutton Hoo, Suffolk, England.
>
> I think high-school and college students should be aware of the new resources that Internet brings to us and that it is useful just to hang out on the net to learn your way around.

REFLECTIONS

We contacted Marcia to pursue her thoughts about using the Internet for learning. We understood that, like many university students, her interests were focused on research and that the newsgroup provided lots of replies to her query. But we were curious about the impact she thought this had on her learning. Was it mostly the access to information she was interested in? The exchanges with others? It turned out to be a bit of both.

"I think the basic thing about the Internet is the accessibility to information and experts in various fields that helps students. Some of the information given to me has not even been published here in Canada yet, which enables me to do better on an essay than someone relying on the library."

Marcia learned to use the Internet at school. While we were impressed by that, we were even more impressed by her thoughts about the importance of *using* her abilities to involve herself in learning:

> I knew a lot about the Internet from my computer classes and articles but until using it to find research information, I don't really believe I understood the impact that global accessibility can have on our educational system. The fact that so much information is just a few key strokes away blows my mind. It's a lot easier to remember things such as facts about an archaeology site when you learn them from people who were actually there. It makes the whole learning experience more interesting and fascinating. It definitely beats having someone teach right from a text-book and not really understanding what they are lecturing about.

As it happens, Marcia contacted us recently to let us know that her online work continued in a course on "Anthropology and the Aboriginal Peoples of Canada" at Trent.

> The purpose of the class was to learn about the conflicts between First Nations peoples and anthropology, and to discuss ways in which things are currently changing within the field. For this purpose we were each assigned a professional to correspond with (i.e., a professor or museum professional.)

By corresponding with these people we were able to learn about their current work with First Nations peoples, and their views on the various issues we covered in class. This project enabled the voices of eighteen people to be heard within our classroom discussions even though there were only nine of us in the class.

To complete the project we each wrote a report on our correspondences and gave a presentation in front of the class on our "professional's" current work. This whole course was fantastic because it enabled students to hear from professionals outside of our own school as well as from our professor at Trent.

Josef

At twenty-four, Josef Hnojil is a Ph.D. student at the Department of Mapping and Cartography, Faculty of Civil Engineering, Czech Technical University in Prague. Not only does he credit the Internet with having had a huge impact on his studies, but he also considers the things he has learned through the Internet indispensable:

My first encounter with the Internet was in a voluntary seminar in the autumn, 1994. It has changed my life. I will never forget about the first contacts with email, Telnet, FTP and Gopher and their possibilities. Working with these services is now automatic to me, so I can concentrate on the content.

Like most of us, Josef found that electronic mail changed the way he communicates, both with friends and colleagues, but there are other changes that Internet usage made to his studies:

In 1995, I began to work with new operating system LINUX, where with help of LaTeX typographic system I wrote my diploma work. Nowadays, I can connect through it to our Supercomputing Centre, where I work with AVS, the visualization system I described with my graduate supervisor, in Chapter 24.

But there are some things that Josef worries about when it comes to using the Internet:

I am quite an Internet enthusiast, but there are some things I am afraid about. Although there are many opportunities to get lessons and read books about the Internet, some people do not know enough about how to control their behavior online, which some people call *netiquette.*

Still, issues like these, online junk mail, the increasing use of the Internet for advertising, and so on, do not overshadow the value Josef feels Internet learning has made to him.

"At last," he writes, "I think it is not important what programs you work with. The most important thing about learning on the Internet to me is that it represents 'information freedom.'

Ilda

Like Marcia, Ilda Carreiro King, a Boston College graduate student, also found the Internet placed her in direct communication with experts, and that it was this link that developed her ideas about what research means—and just who a "colleague" is as well.

I began using email in 1992, while taking a statistics class. Upon discovering that I could communicate with other universities through the Internet, I began communicating with friends and family at other institutions. My use and interest expanded when I began my doctoral studies. At that time I began to create mini-networks within the college for classes so we could discuss material from class and readings as well as perform the more clerical side of sending notices or setting up appointments.

The real power of the Internet did not unfold for me until last March when a professor handed me a communication from the group online discussion based at the Laboratory for the Comparison of Human Cognition out of the University of California at San Diego. A prominent researcher in areas I was exploring was asking the same question I was attempting to address in a paper for which I had had little result in references. I was immediately excited and asked if she could send me any future communications on the topic. She suggested I just join myself. The thought had never occurred to me. I thought you had to be invited to join such high-level discussions. I tentatively joined and really became a junkie immediately, intoxicated by the realization that I was listening to well-respected educators and theorists whom I had read but never dreamed of relating to on a personal level.

REFLECTIONS

Ilda's encounter with changes in "status" between participants provides an excellent example of the "changing roles" we looked at in Chapter 3. The impact of *involvement* and *participation* on the idea of what "research" is allowed her to think about her own work in new ways during her studies:

> As the discussion unfolded I had a real sense of how research develops since it was evident that no one had many answers. The messages seemed to really emulate discussion and I began to feel more like a participant in a conversation. I was pleased that I had chosen seemingly a "cutting-edge" topic for inquiry, but now wanted to ask my specific questions to see if I could generate any direction for my own work.

What Ilda's experience brings to light is how being a participant in a conversation about her research meant that the evolving conversation could *become part of her research* as well. When she realized this, she began to include others in the *development stages* of her ideas:

"I formulated a summary of my project… (and) sent it to the general discussion forum asking for input and references. I received my first reply that day and within two weeks had over twenty contacts across the nation representing a variety of efforts. To my astonishment, I exchanged messages with internationally prominent members of the field of inquiry."

In Closing

Your own situation may be reflected in one or other of the stories we have highlighted from Monica, Marcia, Josef, or Ilda, or perhaps in the projects described here. But even if that isn't the case now, once you are actually on the Internet yourself, it certainly can be.

As you can see, many, many opportunities and examples await you there. After all, the learning highway is a place where collisions are *supposed* to happen—and we hope they will cause you to wonder even more.

Index